ANNA'S 1918 HOME FRONT DIARY

*With Annotations About Oswin Percival Rands, Her Future Husband
Who Was Serving in the U.S. Army in France*

ANNA'S 1918 HOME FRONT DIARY

With Annotations About Oswin Percival Rands, Her Future Husband
Who Was Serving in the U.S. Army in France

Transcribed, Footnoted, and Illustrated
by
RICHARD D. RANDS, A GRANDSON

SUNSTONE
PRESS
SANTA FE

Sunstone books may be purchased for educational, business, or sales promotional use.
For information please write: Special Markets Department, Sunstone Press,
P.O. Box 2321, Santa Fe, New Mexico 87504-2321.

Book and cover design › R. Ahl
Printed on acid-free paper
∞
eBook 978-1-61139-622-5

Library of Congress Cataloging-in-Publication Data

Names: Rands, Richard D., 1943- author.
Title: Anna's 1918 home front diary / Richard D. Rands.
Description: Santa Fe, NM : Sunstone Press, [2020] | Includes index. |
  Summary: "A memoir based on the personal diary of a 20-year-old woman
  during 1918 covering her courtships, her friendships, and her volunteer
  efforts on the home front, culminating with her struggle with an
  influenza pandemic"-- Provided by publisher.
Identifiers: LCCN 2021009683 | ISBN 9781632933195 (paperback) | ISBN
  9781611396225 (epub)
Subjects: LCSH: Lund, Anna, 1898-1989--Diaries. | Lund, Anna,
  1898-1989--Childhood and youth. | Lund, Anna, 1898-1989--Friends and
  associates. | Influenza Epidemic, 1918-1919--Utah--Salt Lake
  City--Personal narratives. | Salt Lake City (Utah)--Biography. | Fort
  Douglas (Utah)--Biography. | LCGFT: Diaries. | Biographies.
Classification: LCC F834.S253 R36 2020 | DDC 979.2/258--dc23
LC record available at https://lccn.loc.gov/2021009683

WWW.SUNSTONEPRESS.COM

SUNSTONE PRESS / POST OFFICE BOX 2321 / SANTA FE, NM 87504-2321 /USA
(505) 988-4418 / FAX (505) 988-1025

Dedication: To Janet Brigham, my wife and editor extraordinaire.

Most of the footnotes and illustrations have been extracted from the following sources:

The Salt Lake Tribune

The Deseret News

Goodwin's Weekly Newspaper

Wikimedia Commons

Google Images

Young Women's Journal

R. L. Polk's City Directory for 1918

Rexburg Standard

Idaho State Historical Society

Utah State Historical Society

Order of Battle of the United States Land Forces in the World War; American Expeditionary Forces: Divisions, Volumes 2 and 3

Combat Service of Organizations of the US Army in the World War

Thru the War with Our Outfit, Being a Historical Narrative of the 107th Ammunition Train, by John C. Acker

Anna at 20 years old.

Born 16 April 1898 at Ogden, Weber, Utah
Married 17 March 1921 at Salt Lake City, Salt Lake, Utah
Died 9 February 1989 at Glendora, Los Angeles, California

CONTENTS

Introduction

The United States entered the Great World War (WWI) in April 1917; a worldwide influenza pandemic invaded Salt Lake City, Utah, in 1918. Fort Douglas, at the eastern edge of Salt Lake City, was to become a major mobilization and training site for the western part of the United States, as well as a German prisoner-of-war camp. A few miles east of the city center, the fort was a relic of the Civil War, originally created to protect the mail routes and telegraph lines to the east. Up to the beginning of the U.S. involvement in WWI, Fort Douglas served as a mobilization site for the Spanish-American War and for skirmishes along the border with Mexico.

Fort Douglas was in the right place at the right time when it was clear that tens of thousands of troops would need to mobilize and train to fight the war in Europe. Teenage Anna Lund, later to become my grandmother, also was in the right place at the right time, as Utah envisioned the godsend the war would be to the state's economy.

When the U.S. declared war on Germany, Anna had just turned 19, born in April 1898 in Ogden, Utah, 40 miles north of Salt Lake City. She was the fourth child of nine. Her father was a Norwegian immigrant whose parents had converted to the Mormon Church (The Church of Jesus Christ of Latter-day Saints, hereafter referred to as LDS or *Mormon Church*) and joined the many thousands of Scandinavian families who gathered to its headquarters, Salt Lake City, in the late 1800s.

Prior to her father's family coming to America, they had opted to drop their patronymic surname of *Hansen* and assume a fixed surname taken from the name of the farm where they lived—*Lunde*. When they arrived in Utah, they settled on the spelling of *Lund*. Grandma's maiden name was Anna Elizabeth Lund. In her later life she occasionally used the name *Anne*, but we do not have her birth certificate to determine which is her formal name. Her father struggled to make a living as a cabinet maker and later as a postal service worker.

Her mother's ancestors, who immigrated from England and the Isle of Man, had also converted to Mormonism, crossed the Atlantic, and trekked from New Orleans to Salt Lake City in the mid-1800s. Anna lived at home as a young adult but built her own life; I wondered, was it unusual for a young woman in the early 1900s to be so independent? She was the oldest child left at home and was, perhaps, in a position of being as little burden as possible on her parents. Among my family documents is an account written by one of Anna's future daughters-in-law, who knew Anna's mother well. She wrote that Anna's mother was not happy and "lived separately in the same house." Such a disjointed family life is not apparent in Anna's writing but may explain her unmistakably self-sufficient nature.

As for her level of education, I have only been able to find her listed as graduating from the eighth grade in June 1912 from nearby Emerson School. I have yet to discover evidence showing her graduating from any further public school. In any case, her writing skills reflect more than an eighth-grade education.

Anna's motivation to start keeping a daily diary at the beginning of 1918 is unknown. The first entry indicates that she has been confined to home, unable to celebrate New Year's Day because of recently having her tonsils removed. But the next day she is off and running with energetic activities, going to work and to a movie as if nothing could slow her down. She encounters an "old friend in uniform," giving us the important clue that she enjoys the presence of unattached military men from all over the country. What is amazing about her account is that she rarely manifests any sign of being cocky.

Anna's writing raises many questions I have tried to resolve. Foremost is the issue of transportation. She regularly goes to work, comes home, and then goes back downtown for school or entertainment, only once mentioning catching a trolley car. At first glance, one would conclude that she walked everywhere she went. It turns out Salt Lake City had a well-developed trolley system that would have been convenient for her.

She readily writes about the man she loves and the ones she dislikes, but she never mentions any degree of intimacy in her relationships. When the man she loves writes to announce his marriage to someone else, she packs up all his "soft" stuff and ships it back to him.

It baffles me that she was so matter-of-fact about the war going on overseas. Despite battles here and there, advances and retreats, she expresses no real evidence of engagement in the horrors. Likewise, she had nothing to say about her two little brothers who had died young, one of scarlet fever at 16 months, the other three days after a complicated birth. Of course, the available space in the small diary was limited, making it difficult to write very much about feelings. That's what makes her diary so amazing: It covers so much in so little space about a momentous year when the United States was deeply involved in a worldwide war and in the midst of a worldwide pandemic.

I have uncovered the history of her eventual husband, Oswin "Dutch" Rands. What I know about his experiences in the trenches of France during 1918 is interwoven with Anna's diary entries, to contrast her life with that of her future husband.

Richard Rands
September 2020
Auburn, California

PROLOGUE
THE DIVING BELLE

Although I wasn't aware of it at first, my paternal grandmother had a significant impact on me when I was a little boy. Within months after I was born, she invited my mother to bring me to Inglewood, California, to live with her while my father—one of her three sons—was overseas during World War II (WWII). Grandma worked as a court clerk. When Dad came home from the war, he was eventually hired to work in the Mojave Desert at Muroc Air Force Base (AFB), now known as Edwards AFB. My parents, my siblings, and I frequently made the several-hour drive over the mountains to Los Angeles to visit grandma at her little house near the end of East Beach Street in Inglewood for holidays and family gatherings. To me, it was a delightful place to visit with a hill out back to climb, tall eucalyptus trees, and a big nearby park and playground. In contrast, when we moved off-base to a small mining town called Boron, our rock house in the desert had sand—nothing but sand, scorpions, and snakes.

In the fall of 1949, Dad decided to use the G.I. Bill to get a college degree at the University of Southern California in Los Angeles. Grandma, who by then had remarried, invited us to live in her house in Inglewood while she and her husband moved a few miles away to South Gate. I remember visiting Grandma even more since she was by then close by, except it was not as fun. She lived on a boulevard so busy that it was too dangerous for us to venture outdoors. My only pleasant memories of Grandma's house involved reading the classic comic books she kept in the wooden basket beside her rocking chair. I still remember being enthralled by stories such as *A Tale of Two Cities* and *King Solomon's Mines*.

At that time, I was much too young to be interested in Grandma's younger years. In later years, I learned what a plucky, self-confident woman she had been, having raised children during the Depression years. After she and her first husband, Grandpa Dutch, divorced, she had a job that paid just barely enough to care for her, my dad, and his two brothers.

One of my favorite stories about Grandma describes an event that took place when she was 19 years old. In front of the Pantages Theatre in downtown Salt Lake City, a Captain Louis Sorcho had set up a large, somewhat portable 15,000-gallon water tank on the busy sidewalk. He was demonstrating his deep-sea diving bell and drumming up interest in his undersea movie, both while recruiting for the U.S. Navy.

Captain Louis Sorcho, submarine engineer, designed this traveling show and recruitment center, here displayed in front of a theater in Calgary, Alberta, Canada, in 1917.

The Captain invited some brave bystander to come forward and don the diving suit with its heavy "iron and brass bell weighing several hundred pounds." The brave bystander who accepted the invitation was my future grandma.

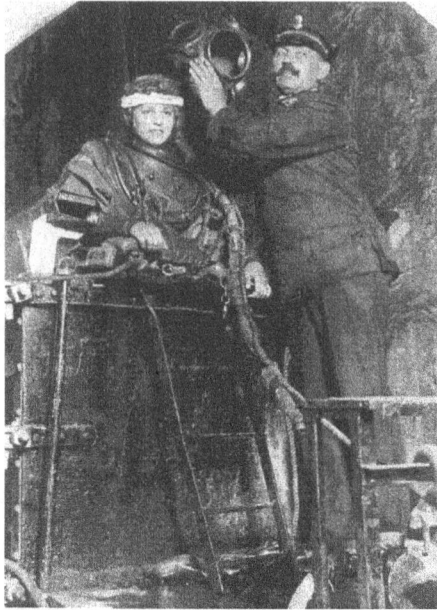

Anna Lund volunteers to try Captain Sorcho's diving bell, Salt Lake City, Utah, 13 July 1917.

One of the recent innovations to diving bells at that time was the addition of a battery-powered telephone. So what did Grandma do? She telephoned the governor of the State of Utah and said, "This is Anna Lund, and I am talking to you from beneath tons of water in the tank at Pantages Theatre." A newspaper article reported that "she had a conversation with the governor, he complimented her on her bravery, and invited her to call on him at the capitol.[1]" It's possible that she might have been drawn to the diving exhibition by good-looking sailor boys standing around.

For unknown reasons, Grandma Anna decided to keep a daily diary during the following year, 1918. After many years, the little book ended up in my possession; my dad concluded that I would be diligent in bringing it to life. I found it to be a charming commentary on the life of a 20-year-old girl in the midst of a city virtually overrun with young soldiers preparing to be sent to war in France. Toward the end of the diary, she described coping with the pandemic of the 1918 influenza.

This is the transcription of the personal diary of Anna Elizabeth Lund for the year 1918 as written in her own hand in a small (3" x 5") black simulated-leather Excelsior Diary. The first 28 pages contain miscellaneous information usually found in almanacs, such as postage rates, a church calendar, astronomical events, weights and measures, weather patterns, lists of Presidents, major cities, first aid, and antidotes for poisons. The first page of the actual diary section is titled "Things Easily Forgotten" and provides space to list personal details, including such items as the number of a watch case or a bank account; weight; height; and sizes of a hat, gloves, hosiery, shoes, drawers, and a skirt.

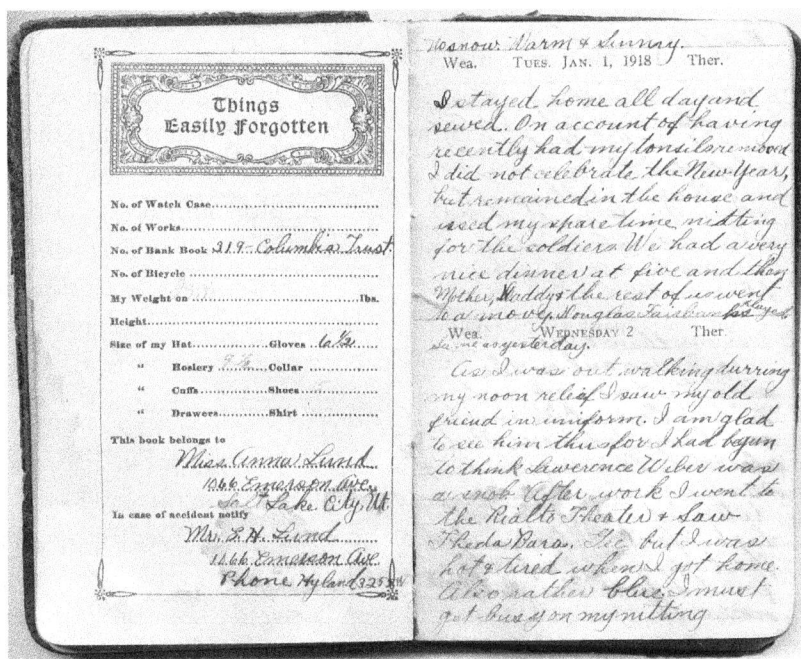

The beginning diary pages of Anna's diary.

On this page is the identification that the book belongs to Anna Lund at 1066 Emerson Avenue, Salt Lake City, Utah, and in case of accident, notify E. H. Lund (Emil Hans Lund, her father), also residing at 1066 Emerson Avenue, phone Hyland 3255W. It also notes that her bank account was 319 at Columbia Trust[2], her weight in January was 111 lbs., her glove size was 6 ½, hosiery size was 9 ½, and her shoe size was 5.

The diary has two days per page, with room at the top of each day for a short note about the weather and the temperature. The line for the date on each section is different and is entered in the transcription as it appears in the diary. At the end of the book are extra pages for some notes, a telephone directory, and some cash account records. Anna often gives a brief description of the weather but only twice records the temperature.

The family home at 1066 Emerson, Salt Lake City, was located between 10th East and 11th East, and Emerson Avenue is equivalent to 1490 South. Probably only people who have spent time in Utah will be able to make the slightest sense of the way streets there are numbered or named.

Anna's occasional mention of attending school in the evening refers to stenography and typing classes she attended at Heneger's Business College at 49 South Main (about a block away from her place of employment), where she enrolled on 19 November 1917. Her references to going to work each weekday for much of the year refer to employment for a dentist, Dr. Ernest A Tripp[3]. She occasionally mentions making trips to parts of the city for him (see March 19) and assisting in setting a broken jaw (see February 8). Her expenses at the end of the diary indicate a weekly receipt of $6 in salary[4]. In a 1918 city directory, Anna is listed as an assistant to E. A. Tripp, whose office is listed at 501 Atlas Blk. (34-38 West 2nd South).

It is not clear from Anna's references to her work for Dr. Tripp exactly what her job entailed. Indeed, the dental profession in 1918 was very much in evolution. I have not been able to determine if Dr. Tripp had been trained in a formal dental school or if he had simply learned the necessary skills working as a dental assistant and then declared himself to be a dentist. The 1918 Salt Lake City directory lists more than 120 dentists. Anna refers to assisting with a dental procedure only once. The fact that she did not pursue a career as a dental assistant or hygienist suggests that she may have aspired to be involved in a business environment. The overall information I derive from the diary is that Anna was not a trained dental assistant, nor did she work a full 40-hour week.

Salt Lake City, Utah

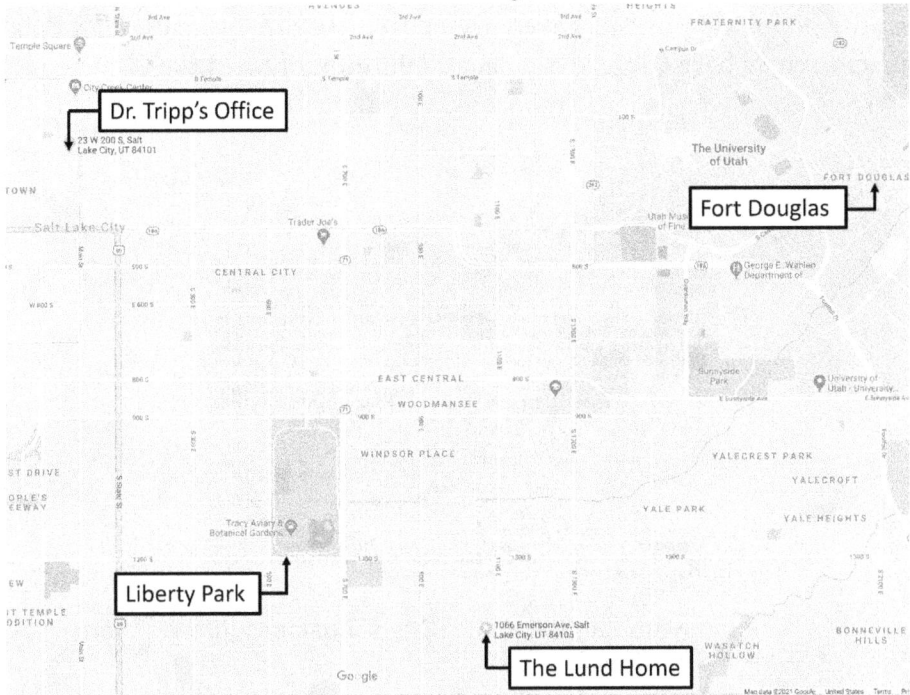

A map of modern Salt Lake City showing the location of the Lund residence relative to the downtown area of the city. The Lund home is at the bottom center, and Anna's downtown place of employment at Dr. Tripp's office is at the upper left, two blocks south of the city center. The distance would have been 3.6 miles on the streets. Between Anna's home and her workplace is Liberty Park, mentioned frequently throughout her diary. Fort Douglas, at the upper right, plays a pivotal role in Anna's story.

On 26 November 1918, at the end of her diary, Anna begins her first day at a new job with the Dodge Brothers Co., which appears to be a vacuum cleaner company. At first she is leery about the position because she is bored, but soon she becomes more comfortable as she picks up more responsibilities, including selling vacuum cleaners.

The 1918 edition of R. L. Polk's *City Directory* for Salt Lake City reported that regardless of more than 5,000 men serving in the U.S. military services, the directory listed 71,951 individual names for 1918. The directory surmised this as a sign that Salt Lake City "shows a healthy and substantial growth in population." The directory further claims that

Polk's rough estimate was a bit optimistic. The official population records list the population in Salt Lake City in 1920 as 116,110, although Polk's directory may have adopted a broader definition of Salt Lake City.

Simultaneous with that growth has come general strength-ening of business conditions. Industries of Salt Lake City every day are falling into the war efficiency stride in a manner known to delight those of substantial advancement in the commercial world. Salt Lake's response to the Liberty loan, Red Cross and War Savings drives is a source for great pride.

The increased advertising and subcription patronage of the 1918 directory of Salt Lake City gives definite testimony to the steady business growth. Certain business changes have taken place, but, only to make way for big industries which the war will demand and which will mean a much larger popula-tion for Salt Lake.

Destined to important local expansion the steel industry, which is developing steadily in Salt Lake City, ultimatley will add hundreds of happy and prosperous families to the City. Other industries are gaining and soon Fort Douglas, the University of Utah and other temples of learning will be scenes of extensive actual preparation of young men for the battle fields of Europe. These activities will contribute generally to the stimulation of trade conditions.

Contained within the boards of this directory are the names of 71,951 persons. Multiply this number by 2 (the average number of persons allotted to each family) and Salt Lake City (including its adjacent surburban territory) will be found to have 143,902 inhabitants. The estimate is confined to actual residents and does not include transoients.

Comment about Salt Lake City's business growth from R. L. Polk's *City Directory*.

The Lund family would have been members of the Emerson Ward (a church congregation) of the Granite Stake (a group of wards) of The Church of Jesus Christ of Latter-day Saints (Mormon), which was the predominant religion in the area. The place of worship for the Emerson Ward was located at 1051 Emerson Avenue, within the same block but across the street from the Lund family home. Emil Hans Lund, Anna's father, was a carrier for the U.S. Postal Service.

Anna occasionally was listed in the society pages of the Salt Lake City newspapers leading up to 1917, when she was hosting receptions and parties for friends and family members, suggesting that she was popular in her social circle and that her family was known in the community. By 1917 Anna was old enough to seek serious employment and appears to have discontinued her hosting activities. The event shown below was a reception for her future sister-in-law, Ruby Fredrickson, who married Anna's older brother Leander (Le) on 2 September 1916.

The Salt Lake Herald-Republican, Salt Lake City, Utah, 13 August 1916, page 25.

It seems clear that Anna was not writing her diary to be read by someone else. Many details are vague and difficult to decipher. Reference to many acquaintances are by first names only. A few are listed at the back, but even then, they are essentially anonymous. Some of the soldiers were from unknown cities. In 1918, Salt Lake City was a medium-size city with a cohesive population.

I hope some readers will relish the chance to delve into some of the mysteries that I have not been able to resolve. It will be great fun to have readers tell me that their grandfather mentioned fighting alongside someone who wrote to Anna Lund, or that Lawrence Weber was probably their grandfather because... I expect sequels to this story. For example, she mentions a dear friend who died; learning more about their friendship could lead to another chapter in Anna's story.

The United States was a formal participant in the Great World War (WWI) from 6 April 1917 until the war's end on 11 November 1918, and afterward in the Army of Occupation in 1919. As a result, many of Anna's male friends were in the military during the early part of the diary. Fort Douglas, located a few miles east of downtown Salt Lake City, was by 1918 the focal point for tens of thousands of troops being mobilized and trained for duty in France and other battlefields. Anna's diary reveals her sense of responsibility toward making their sojourn in Salt Lake City as friendly as possible.

Fort Douglas, as seen looking southwest across the Salt Lake Valley, ca. 1920.

As part of the American population's obligation to support the war effort, a constant push was made to get everyone to purchase war savings bonds and stamps, support the Red Cross, and other means to help the government pay for the war. Anna considered it her duty to participate, and according to the monthly expense records at the back of the diary, she pledges $5 per month for seven months and records payments from January through July where she notes "finished."

Grandpa "Dutch"

Among the many soldiers she mentions is Oswin Rands (see diary entry for 29 March), "an old time would be sweet heart" who was my grandfather-to-be. Her reference to Oswin in such a dismissive manner gives the diary a curious air. I know little about the circumstances prior to 1918 when he apparently attempted to court Anna, or about the situation after his return in early 1919 that led to their marriage nearly two and a half years later.

Oswin's military service record has not been available because many of the Army records were destroyed or damaged in a fire at the National Military Personnel Records Center at St. Louis, Missouri, in 1973. Restoration teams are currently undertaking a major effort to salvage what they can, and until that record becomes available, if at all, what we know of Oswin's military service is extracted from other military records and newspapers; these are interleaved chronologically in Anna's diary indented as a contrast to her daily life.

Finding Oswin's WWI Draft Registration record or any enlistment record has been challenging. Initially, I assumed that he registered in Ogden, Utah, where his two older brothers, Joseph Leslie Rands and William

Clayton Rands, registered. They registered together on 5 June 1917, but an extensive initial search of military records, newspapers, and other sources failed to uncover Oswin's entry into the military for WWI. However, a chance discovery in a document titled the *U.S., Adjutant General Military Records for Idaho, 1917–1918*, listed Oswin P. Rands among members of Company M in the National Guard of Idaho. Company M of the 2nd Idaho Infantry was the unit initially recruited from a town called Emmett, a few miles north of Boise, but later included enlisted men from the towns of Blackfoot, Rexburg, and Idaho Falls. That discovery changed the focus of my search from Utah to Idaho.

From my family history research experience, I knew that the Rands family had deep connections with the business community in Rexburg, Madison County, and with the Mormon Church, particularly with the local church school, Ricks Academy, in Rexburg. At the end of the Adjutant General's record is an alphabetical list of registrations by county. When I turned to the section for Madison County and skipped to the Rs, I found the entry for *Rands, Oswell*—evidently a misspelling of *Oswin*. Unfortunately, the record listed only his year of registration, not the full month and day. But now, at least, I knew *where* Oswin likely had joined the military.

My next step was to go back through the draft registration records focusing on those from Idaho. But to no avail. That's when I decided to retrace newspapers from Idaho to look for announcements of draft and enlistments between 1917 and 1918. From experience, I knew that newspapers occasionally listed the names of men serving from their towns long after they had joined. Searching the site NewspaperArchive.com, I found that the Rands name appears often in Idaho, but when I reached the articles in April 1917, when war was declared, I saw this headline in the *Rexburg Standard*, "Seventeen Rexburg Boys Enlist in Company M." The date of the article was Thursday, April 5, and the story indicated that the "boys" had enlisted the previous Sunday (April 1), and had entrained for Idaho Falls that evening, where they were to be combined with those from other towns and sent on their way to Boise, where the Idaho National Guard was headquartered.

The article listed the names of the seventeen Rexburg boys, which included *Osborn Rands*, again a misspelling of Oswin's name. I needed to pinpoint what Oswin was doing in Rexburg when he joined, instead of joining in Ogden, where his brothers had enlisted. Oswin's two brothers were living and working in Ogden in 1917, but Oswin's family was still living in Rexburg until the end of 1919, when his father, Hyrum, sold his confectionery store and moved his family to live with children in Ogden. I found a newspaper article that reported some years later that Hyrum had taken his family through Rexburg on their way to Yellowstone Park, and he was referred to as an "old pioneer in the community and operated the first hotel in Rexburg." Another article mentioned that Hyrum had been interviewed by a famous western novelist, Owen Wister[5], for material to write his novels, including *The Virginian*.

For months after the declaration of war, Idaho newspapers describe the mustering of enlisted men throughout Idaho to fill out the ranks of each of the companies, including Company M, which reached full war strength by 7 April. Newspapers mention a company of about thirty men who were recruited from all over Idaho to be what was called a *machine gun battalion*. Such a battalion was typically assigned to a division, but the 2nd Infantry in Idaho was not large enough to be considered a division.

The initial thirty men of the Idaho machine gun battalion found themselves to be an "orphaned company," meaning they were not attached to a specific battalion and did not have a town or county as their sponsor. They had no one to send them goodies, special supplies, or equipment, or to champion their cause in parades. Since Oswin eventually shipped off to France as part of a machine gun battalion, he may have been part of this group. The orphaned machine gun unit of Idaho's 2nd Infantry was quickly adopted by a small group of businessmen and provided with all the amenities given the other companies.

The Idaho 2nd Infantry National Guard at the Boise Barracks in 1917.

Even though the machine gun had been invented thirty years earlier, it had not been used heavily in war until WWI. It had evolved into a lightweight, rapid-fire armament that drastically changed how war was fought. When the Idaho 2nd Infantry was instructed by the U.S. Army to create a machine gun unit, it wasn't yet clear how the unit would fit into the normal military organization. These men were trained differently; they required different ammunition, were less mobile than infantry and cavalry, and were deployed separately in battle. Eventually, the machine-gun battalions were grouped with the engineer and medical companies, the ammunition trains, the artillery units, and the band. The entire collection of special units was joined together into a "headquarters company," which seemed to satisfy the U.S. Army's need for an orderly chain of command.

At one point, Oswin's outfit was sent north for guard duty to Camp George Wright, located just west of the Idaho border near Spokane, Washington. The fort was named after an infamous, merciless U.S. Army colonel who proudly slaughtered Native Americans. Wright allowed some of his conquered enemies to come into camp to make peace, and then he arrested and summarily executed many of them without even a pretense of trial.

As indicated above, Oswin enlisted in Company M of the Idaho National Guard, but when the guard was transferred to the U.S. military, the unit designation changed, and the soldiers were reassigned to different units. Drawing from the publication *Order of Battle of the United States Land Forces in the World War, American Expeditionary Forces: Divisions* Volume 2, (pp. 257, 267-269), we see that the National Guard troops of six Western states, including Idaho, were drafted into federal service on 5 August 1917, designated to form the 41st Division, and sent to Camp Kearny, Linda Vista, California (near San Diego), for training. Reorganizations and redesignations occurred, but the record indicates that the 41st Division embarked for Europe in groups beginning as early as 26 July 1917, with all units arriving in England by 31 August 1917, well before Oswin shipped out for France.

The first military record showing him in active service is an Army Transport embarkation passenger list dated 11 January 1918, for transport ship No. 527. Subsequent documents indicate that No. 527 was the HMT *Olympic* (HMT, His Majesty's Transport), a sister ship to the RMS *Titanic* (RMS, Royal Majesty's Ship). The *Olympic* had been built in the Belfast, Ireland, shipyard alongside the *Titanic* but was launched after the ill-fated

Titanic. Many of the enhancements learned from the failure of the *Titanic* had been implemented into the *Olympic*.

The HMT *Olympic* in dazzle camouflage during WWI; dazzle was a disruptive camouflage technique designed to confuse rather than conceal.

Oswin is listed as a wagoner in the Headquarters Company of the 41st Division, 146th Machine Gun Battalion, departing from New York. Apparently, at some point before July, Oswin was assigned to the 41st Division and was attached to the 146th Machine Gun Battalion, which was part of the Division Headquarters Troop, consisting of 198 officers and 5,454 enlisted men. Some evidence indicates that the 41st Division was sent to Fort Greene, North Carolina, for its final training, and then to Camp Mills, New York, before embarkation for France.

Some units of the 41st were aboard the SS *Tuscania* in February 1918 when it was torpedoed by a German U-boat and sunk off the coast of Northern Ireland. Oswin was already in France. (I certainly can say that deciphering highly codified military documents can be a challenge to a layperson.)

After Oswin arrived in France, at the port of Brest, the only official document of his whereabouts was a bimonthly muster roll of Company A of the 107th Ammunition Train from 30 April to 30 June 1918. The remarks beside his name are "Transferred as Wagoner fr[om] Wagoner per SO 89, Ex. 3, HQ 57th F.A Brigade June 13/18." One other wagoner on the same muster roll has the same remarks. I am hopeful that his official service record (DD-214) will someday become available and will reveal the details of his assignments. Until then, for the purpose of this account, I assume that he was transferred to 107th Ammunition Train of the Headquarters Company of the 41st Division on 13 June 1918. Oswin was listed as a member of the 107th in the roster of the *Historical Narrative of the 107th Ammunition Train*, a detailed log by John C. Acker. The events pertaining to Oswin's experiences in France that are intertwined with Anna's diary are based largely on the history by Acker.

Included here is a list of Anna's immediate family, with Anna listed as *Daughter*, to help the reader follow her use of family names and nicknames (only marriages in effect in 1918 are listed, with relationships to the parents Emil Hans and Laura Lucretia):

Father: Emil Hans Lund ("Daddy"), born 22 January 1866, Frederickstad, Ostfold, Norway; died 8 June 1946, Salt Lake City, Utah

Mother: Laura Lucretia Partington ("Mother"), born 16 May 1869, Logan, Utah; died 25 March 1958, Los Angeles, California

Son: Halvor Allan Lund ("Hal"), born 6 April 1891, Salt Lake City, Utah; died 19 February 1959, Los Angeles; married Lauretta Margaret Greenwell ("Laura")

Son: Leander Emil Lund ("Le"), born 20 October 1892, Salt Lake City; died 14 June 1925, Los Angeles; married Ruby LaVern Frederickson

Son: William Edward Lund ("Billy" or "Billy Boy"), born 26 December 1895, Ogden, Utah; died 10 April 1982, Salt Lake City; married Ruby Rosetta Fisher

Daughter: Anna Elizabeth Lund, born 16 April 1898, Ogden; died 9 February 1989, Glendora, California

Daughter: Laura Andrea Lund ("Lal"), born 1 November 1901, Salt

Lake City; died 3 August 1991, Salt Lake City

Daughter: Violet Lund ("Vi" and "Viol"), born 10 December 1904, Salt Lake City; died 16 November 2003, Farmington, Utah

Son (deceased young): Quayle Ulyses Lund, born 22 August 1907, Salt Lake City; died 16 February 1909, Salt Lake City

Son (deceased young): Paul Partington Lund, born 15 July 1910, Salt Lake City; died 17 July 1910, Salt Lake City

Son: Donald True Lund ("Don"), born 17 August 1911, Salt Lake City; died 25 March 2003, Mesa, Arizona

The Transcription

Editor's note: According to rules of historical transcription, I am expected to leave the spelling and punctuation as Anna wrote it, which I have done in most cases. However, in a few places, I have made corrections (marked with brackets [ ] and less frequently braces { } to ensure clarity). Whenever possible, I have identified individuals in my comments or footnotes.

My comments (indented) appear after some of the entries.

For a list of the names of Anna's acquaintances and their possible information, see her address list at the end of the diary.

1

JANUARY

SEWING, KNITTING, MOVIES, AND HOPE FOR PEACE

Celebrating New Year's Eve and New Year's Day in 1918 was a bit unusual, especially in Salt Lake City. The war was staggering but unnervingly distant because of severe censorship. Celebrations often seemed inappropriate. A prohibition amendment had been proposed to the country and was awaiting ratification.

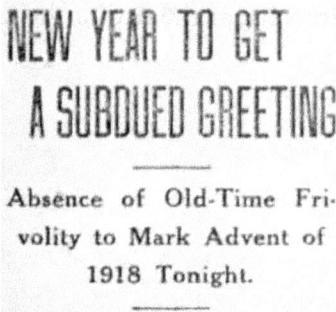

NEW YEAR TO GET A SUBDUED GREETING

Absence of Old-Time Frivolity to Mark Advent of 1918 Tonight.

A subdued New Years Eve, *Salt Lake Tribune*, 31 December 1917, page 10.

The usual "watch parties" were scheduled by the Elks, the Eagles, the Moose, the Masons, and other fraternities and church groups to "watch" the departure of 1917 and the arrival of 1918, but they were expected to be poorly attended that year. It was common for popular restaurants to fully book their tables well in advance for families and groups of friends. This year the bookings were sparse. The newspapers on New Year's Day reported successes on the battle front, deadly freezing temperatures on the East coast of the United States, and the deaths and wounded of Utahns at the war front.

WITH NEW YEAR RUMLESS, ALL EVENTS ARE TRANQUIL

"Quietest in City's History," Is Way Police Describe Day; Less Spectacular Parties Are Enjoyed

A tranquil, rumless New Years Day, *Salt Lake Telegram*,
1 January 1918, page 2.

Although the country hoped for a decent baseball season in 1918, some teams across the nation were calling it quits because so many good players were serving in the military. Schools were being forced to suspend teaching German. Communities in the Midwest, where the population was composed heavily of Germans-from-Russia and their descendants, were being forced to denounce any allegiance to Germany and to raise the American flag.

Anna's opening remarks in her diary reflect a restful day of dutiful work for the war effort, followed by a quiet, celebratory evening at the movies. It appears that her employer had taken time off over the holiday to go deep-sea fishing off the coast of Southern California. His prowess with the fishing pole was in the limelight in the *Salt Lake Tribune* the day before. Perhaps the holiday break in Dr. Tripp's office was the time Anna needed to deal with a problem with her tonsils.

BATTLES GIANT SEA BASS
SALT LAKER IS VICTOR

Dr. E. A. Tripp and His Catch. This Black Sea Bass Weighs 206 Pounds

Dr. E. A. Tripp Lands Fine Specimen in Catalina Island Waters.

Anna's boss takes a holiday fishing expedition to California, *Salt Lake Tribune*, 31 December 1917, page 1.

The stage is now set for Anna's first entry.

Tuesday, 1 January 1918—Weather: No snow. Warm & sunny

I stayed home all day and sewed. On account of having recently had my tonsils removed [on Saturday, 29 December 1917], I did not celebrate the New Year, but remained in the house and used my spare time [k]nitting for the soldiers. We had a very nice dinner at five and then Mother, Daddy & the rest of us went to a movy. Douglas Fairbanks played.[6]

In January 1918, Anna Elizabeth Lund would have been 19 years old and would have had three younger siblings at home with her, Laura, Violet, and Donald. Two older siblings, Halvor and Leander, were already married. William, just older than Anna, was serving in the U.S. Navy aboard the USS *Pittsburgh*. Two younger siblings, Quayle and Paul, had died young.

On this occasion, a movie starring Douglas Fairbanks was playing at the Rialto Theater;[7] it was called *In Again—Out Again* and was about a man who is jilted by his girlfriend and takes to drinking to drown his sorrows. His drunkenness lands him in jail, where he falls for the jailer's daughter. When released, the young man tries everything to get back in jail, where this time he is mistaken for an anarchist bomber. In the end he finds himself facing not just jail but execution.

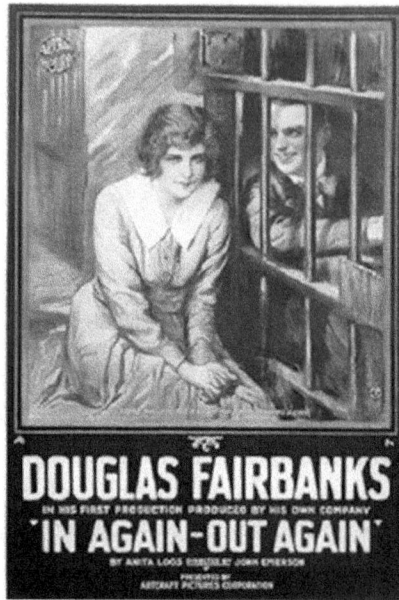

Douglas Fairbanks at the Rialto Theater, *Salt Lake Herald-Republican*, 1 January 1918, page 7.

Knitting for soldiers became a worldwide activity sponsored by countless organizations, including the Red Cross. Many women's suffrage teams switched their attention to knitting, most already knowing how to knit. The painting by Julian Alden Weir below is a touching depiction of a young woman wearing a pretty, white, lacy blouse while knitting for soldiers. Julian's father was painter Robert Walter Weir, a professor of drawing at the military academy at West Point. Anna was known to wear similar white lacy blouses.

Knitting for Soldiers—1918, by Julian Alden Weir (1852–1919).

Of course, some had to learn to knit, prompting the following quip from an Audrey J. Reid, who received the following verse from a New Zealand infantryman:

Life of a pair of socks
They are some fit!
I used one for a helmet
And the other for a mitt
Glad to hear
You're doing your bit—
But who the _____
Said you can knit?!

Wednesday, 2 January 1918—Weather: Same as yesterday

As I was out walking [during] my noon relief I saw my old friend in uniform. I am glad to see him thus for I had begun to think Lawrence Weber was a snob. After work I went to the Rialto Theater & Saw Theda Bara[8]. Gee but I was hot & tired when I got home. Also rather blue. I must get busy on my [k]nitting.

Since Lawrence Weber is an "old friend," I expected to find references to him in local records. Not so. Without more about him, he will just have to remain unexplored. Showing at the Rialto and starring Theda Bara was the movie *Camille*, a chick-flick about a young Parisienne girl in love with a man whose father forbids her from marrying his son. After much ado, Camille becomes poor and stricken with a terminal illness, only to find that the boy still loves her. At two days into the diary, already we can see a trend in Anna's choice of movies.

Thursday, 3 January 1918—Weather: Beautiful & Sunny

Went out walking at noon I met Mrs. [Ada] Byerline[9] & Adelaide [mother & 14-year-old daughter, who lived about half a mile from Anna's home]. I went and helped them shop for they never get any thing in clothing unless they consult me first. They seem to think I am the only one who knows. It makes me feel conceited.

Anna's comments about the warm and sunny weather are further amplified by the clothing store advertisements in the newspapers of the day. They were all announcing drastic clearance sales on excess winter clothing unsold because of the mild winter weather.

Friday, 4 January 1918—Weather: Warmer than ever.

As I was out on the street at noon I met Billie Ernst. He invited me home to dinner. But already had an engagement so we [arranged] for Mon [see January 7]. Attended a meeting with Supts. Lafont & Watson and fixed up an[n]ual report for S. School. I'm glad its over with.

In the 1918 city directory I found a William and Margaret Ernst, but the corresponding census records do not fit the description (an 18-month-old child) mentioned in the diary. Anna was probably the Sunday School secretary in her church congregation and met with the Sunday School superintendents to wrap up the attendance records for 1917.

Saturday, 5 January 1918—Weather: little colder.

Ate lunch with Vivian. Laura & I went to [Bonneville] Park[10] in evening. Had a dandy time. Met some nice fellows among whom were Mess Sargent Emerson, Mr. Beverley a dandy boy & a funny jolly Dutchman named Franklin. He liked me too.

Vivian was Anna's best friend whose name appears frequently throughout the diary as *Viv*. Anna also mentions a Vivian Kuhn for whom she is sewing a dress. It is not clear that Anna's close friend is the same as Vivian Kuhn. A young woman named Bert often is mentioned at the same time as Viv. I have yet to identify Bert, but I suspect she may have been related to Viv.

Laura is Anna's closest younger sister, sometimes referred to as *Lal* (Laura Andrea Lund). She was sixteen years old at this point.

Sunday, 6 January 1918—Weather: Little rain in A.M.

Went to sunday school as usual. Had dinner at five and Mr. Clever & Moore called on Laura & I in evening and we went to church. Very good servi[c]es. I think I like Mr. Clever a little better than at first & he has such beautiful teeth & hair as waivy & heavy as can be.

Monday, 7 January 1918—Weather: Rain all day.

I went out to Billie & Peggy Ernst's place to lunch. Had a delightful time. They have such a sweet captivating jolly little girl 18 mo. old. I got back to work a half hr. late. Saw Douglas Fairbanks after work then went to school. I believe I liked it a little better.

Douglas Fairbanks at the Paramount Theater, *Salt Lake Tribune*, 7 January 1918, page 5.

Tuesday, 8 January 1918—Weather: A little rain & sleet all day. Colder. Nothing of special importance happened. I got a letter from Sergt. Chapla. He wrote a little nicer and still says he loves me and adds that he trusts me too. I returned an ans. letter.

Sergeant John Chapla, of Co. F, 43rd Infantry, Camp Pike, Arkansas (now Savannah, Georgia) was Anna's current number-one boyfriend. Anna's scrapbook has an undated photo of the two of them together.

Anna and Sergeant John Chapla.

Wednesday, 9 January 1918—Weather: Snow & blizzard all day.

I went with Vivian to the American Theater and saw Viola Danna. She surely is cute. Then went to school. When I got home a picture of Jonny was waiting for me. It was very nice of him to send it.

Viola Dana at the American Theater, *Deseret News*, 9 January 1918, page 4.

Viola Dana (Virginia Flugrath) was just one year older than Anna, and had just made a silent film titled *Blue Jeans*, in which, in a melodramatic scene, the unconscious hero is placed on a board approaching a huge buzz saw in a sawmill, "later imitated to the point of cliché," as a modern review notes.

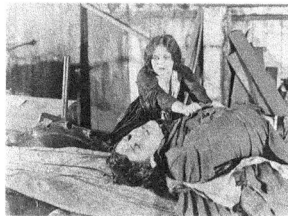

Viola Dana and the Great Sawmill Scene.

The photo Anna received was probably of Sergeant John Chapla.

Thursday, 10 January 1918—Weather: Cold as the dickens today.[11]

The papers are talking of peace. The people in Germany are uprising against the Kaiser. The whole world wants peace. But it seems impossible so soon and only a few months ago it seemed impossible to have war. I hope the dawn of peace will be very soon.

The front page headlines of the major newspapers in Salt Lake City leading up to this day carried stories of peace negotiations being planned, but the front page headline of the *Salt Lake Tribune* on the morning of 7 January declared, "GERMANY HALTS PEACE PARLEY BECAUSE OF RUSSIAN DEMANDS."

Friday, 11 January 1918—Weather: Warmer & snow all Day.

I think this is the jolliest weather we have had for a long time. Mr. Clever phoned last night. I could not see him then but will tonight after school. I did not see him after all. The dirty thing, him. I don't care [though].

Meanwhile, Oswin Rands set sail from New York for France aboard the HMT *Olympic* as part of the 41st Division of the American Expeditionary Force. His unit was the 146th Machine Gun Battalion of the Headquarters Company. The *Olympic* was capable of crossing the Atlantic in about five days.

Saturday, 12 January 1918—Weather: [see below]

2 P.M. It is raining now, but this morning the earth was covered with about seven inches of soft fleecy white, and large flakes were falling. That will spoil the sleighing & skating. I just saw two poor lonely homesick soldiers walk down the street holding hands. I guess they have to love each other. No one else loves them[12].

Sun. January 13, 1918—Weather: Clear Day. Moderately cold.

Last night, Mr. Clever called up & appologized for being late and so I forgave him & went to the Orpheum[13] with him. He thinks I am a widow. I must change that idea quickly. Le & Ruby & Max came to dinner and we had a nice time. I went to [Sunday School] in A.M. as usual.

Orpheum Vaudeville program for the Week of 10 January 1918, *Goodwin's Weekly*, 12 January 1918, page 11.

Le and Ruby were Anna's older brother (by six years), Leander Emil Lund, and his wife. Max is their son, who was five months old.

Monday, 14 January 1918—Weather: [see below] We are having chang[e] able weather again. Clear and then snow & blizzard. Guess I'll go to school again tonight.

Tuesday, 15 January 1918—Weather: [see below] Nothing of special importance. It snowed all day long. About a foot deep in the evening. Adelaide Byerline came down & had her dress fitted. A nice letter from John. They have had orders to prepare to leave any time from Ark[14].

Oswin Rands arrived in France, probably Brest, where most large troop ships docked. The 41st Division was redesignated as the Base and Training Division of the I Corps. A corps base and training division was responsible for the reception, classification, and preliminary training of troops arriving from the United States. Later, the 41st Division received a major disappointment when it was designated a replacement division and never went into combat as a complete unit.

Wednesday, 16 January 1918—Weather:

Uncle Sam has made drastic measures to conserve coal. In the East only five working days are to be had in each week. Went to school. Left at 8:30 I was so tired.

Newspaper accounts mentioned a nationwide effort to reduce the demand for coal, including eliminating nonessential rail cars from trains, and improving efficiency of furnaces and boilers. Passenger trains often included observation cars that were not considered essential. January 30 was declared as National Tag-Your-Shovel Day, and was designated a nationwide school holiday on which children everywhere would go about their cities and towns attaching pre-printed tags to coal shovels with a statement declaring, "Save that Shovelful of coal a day for Uncle Sam." Anna's comment suggests that her home was heated by a coal furnace.

Thursday, 17 January 1918—Weather:

There is not such a great shortage hear as in the East. But as a means of preventing hoarding and waste, no one can buy more than ten lbs. of sugar or 48 lbs. of flowr at one time. Mailed a letter to John. I must resume my studies & knitting.

Friday, 18 January 1918—Weather: Warmer & pleasant.

Carl Atherton took Laura & I to the Orpheum last night. It was a good show. We had lots of fun. I like Carl just fine. I go to school again tonight. Carl phoned in the evening to Laura. He wants me to meet his sheep hearder friend. I like wool growers.

It is sort of amusing that Anna, a dedicated seamstress, thinks of shepherds as wool growers.

Saturday, 19 January 1918—Weather: Warm & Sunny

Went over to the county Bild'g. grownds during noon. Beautiful snow [scenes] over there. Stayed home all evening.

The Salt Lake City and County Building in Downtown Salt Lake City.

Sunday, 20 January 1918—Weather:

Went to Sunday School Convention in Granite Stake at 9A.M. At 2P.M. Laura, Carl Atherton, Mr. Rowe & Myself attended the skiing to[u]rnament. Record jump was 83 ft[15]. Had lots of fun. We met Walter Wills & Mr. Withem. We arrived home at 5:30 just in time for dinner wich was fine after the hike. The boys left at 8:30.

Goes a-Skiing in the Sky
This Is a 73-Foot Jump
Melgard Wins New Honor

Annual Salt Lake Event Is Given Impetus by Success of Yesterday's Contest.

WITH the winning of another leg of the Wandering cup of the N. P. F. Sportslag for ski competition in Salt Lake by 'Axel Andresen of the city yesterday, and the winning of the prize for points by A. Melgard of Spring Valley, Wyo., skiing, the "baby" sport of Salt Lake, received another boost. The ski tournament has become an annual event in Salt Lake, and each year finds

A. Melgard, champion of Wyoming, breaking the Salt Lake record in long jumps at the ski tournament held yesterday. He made a jump of seventy-three feet, which was later beaten by Axel Andresen of Salt Lake. Melgard was point winner at the tournament. He was twenty feet in the air when snapped.

— Photo by Schramm-Johnson Kodak dept.

Annual Ski Jump Tournament at Dry Canyon, *Salt Lake Telegram*, 21 January 1918, page 2.

Monday, 21 January 1918—Weather: Cold and clear.

Received a nice letter from the Serge[a]nt. I went to school at 6 P.M. Wrote him when I returned home. If the weather stays like this there will be skating soon. Little Mildred Merrill died last night; is to be buried today. She was so sweet.

The death certificate for Mildred Merrill indicated that she died of heart complications resulting from diphtheria at age seven. Her family lived on Harrison Avenue, about six blocks from the Lunds. According to the Utah Public Health Association, many midwives unwittingly carried infections from one home to another. Diphtheria wiped out entire families with a death rate of 525 per 100,000. By 1920, a vaccine nearly eradicated diphtheria in the United States.

Tuesday, 22 January 1918—Weather: Cold & grey all day. A few flakes of snow.

I called on Mrs. Merrill after work. Of coarse she feels very badly. It brings back my happy girl hood days when I loved Dorothy so much and she was taken away from us [Anna's dearest friend Dorothy Merrill was the older sister of young Mildred.]

Dorothy Merrill, was a close friend of fifteen-year-old Anna, died on 17 March 1914 at LDS Hospital of heart disease and pneumonia. Anna's scrapbook has a photo of Dorothy and a copy of the funeral description clipped from a newspaper, with the source of the article missing. I have yet to locate the original newspaper source of the clipping. Dorothy's funeral reveals that she was highly regarded in the community and that her family must have been well connected in Mormon leadership. Several high-ranking authorities of the church attended the funeral services, including two members of the Quorum of the Twelve Apostles, and one future apostle and member of the church's First Presidency.

Wednesday, 23 January 1918—Weather:

At noon today I received word from John saying that he had [slipped] and hurt his back. He thinks it is broken but I know better for he couldn't move if it was. I went to school again. I wrote to the Army Hospital about him.

Lovely Dorothy Merrill
Rests on the Hillside

Simple but impressive funeral services for Miss Dorothy Merrill were held at 2 o'clock yesterday afternoon at the Emerson ward chapel. The building was packed to capacity with friends of the young lady and of the family, and beautiful tributes were paid to her memory by several speakers. Fifty girl friends marched in order to the chapel, each bearing a bouquet of flowers which, when placed on the casket, almost concealed it from view.

Bishop George Arbuckle of the ward presided and Elders George Albert Smith and Joseph F. Smith, Jr., of the Council of the Twelve, Bishop Franklin S. Tingey of the Seventeenth ward,

DOROTHY MERRILL.

d Robert T. Taylor, formerly Miss errill's Sunday school teacher, were speakers. D. W. Cummings, her ology teacher at the L. D. S. U., d a poetical tribute written by one Miss Merrill's girl friends at the L. S. U. and the Seventeenth ward uartet sang appropriate selections. Miss Elva Evans, a girl friend, sang "Rest in the Lord." D. W. Cummings offered the invocation, and N. V. Jones pronounced the benediction. Burial was in the city cemetery, where prayers were offered by Stephen L. Richards and Lester Merrill, the latter dedicating the grave; and a song "Nearer, My God, to Thee," was sung by the quartet. The six young pallbearers were three of Miss Merrill's cousins and three of her schoolmates from the L. D. S. U.

Description of Dorothy Merrill's Funeral, 17 Mar 1914, Unknown source, clipping found in Anna's scrapbook.

Thursday, 24 January 1918—Weather: [see below]

Went for a long walk on noon hr. alone. Hurried home after work and sewed on Adelaid's dress. [Arthur and Walter] Wills called up and I received a nice letter from Lauretta. It is so warm & sunny it seems like Spring, that there is still several inches of snow on the grownd.

Lauretta is probably Anna's sister-in-law, Lauretta Greenwell, the wife of Hal. Lauretta later died in 1929 in Los Angeles, California, at the age of 36 from "a general breakdown that followed a severe attack of influenza."

Friday, 25 January 1918—Weather: Very warm & sunny like Spring.

Went to school and typed a hurried letter me[a]nt to cheer the Sargt. Hurried home and went to a dance in the Ward with Arthur & Walter Wills & Laura & another couple. We had a wonderful time. I met a number of new people as well as a lot of old friends. Joh[n]ny Smith was there. Good to see him again.

Saturday, 26 January 1918—Weather:

Nothing of special importance. "At Last Post." by W.K.E[16]. ["]Come home! Come home! / The winds are at rest in the restful trees; / At rest are the waves of the sundown seas; / And home—they'er home—/ The wearied homes and the broken lives—/ At home! At ease!["] The auther was killed in the trenches.

Sunday, 27 January 1918—Weather: Cold & grey and a little snow.

Went to S.S. as per usual. Mr. Rowe and Carl Atherton visited us in the evening. Had a jolly time. They brought a box of chocolates. I made some candy to send to John. I wish I could know how he is.

Monday, 28 January 1918—Weather:

A letter came from John this A.M. He is improving. His back is badly bruised. I did not attend school, but returned home & sewed. The 43rd infantry is stationed in various places in the Gulf States.

Tuesday, 29 January 1918—Weather: [see below]

Vivian came home with me to dinner. We walked th[r]ough the Park[17]. Was cold but beautiful. Carl phoned and made an appointment for tomorrow. He has been ho[n]orably discharged from the Army for tuberculosis. It is terrible and he is such a dandy boy.

Anna did not specify any details about Carl Atherton except that he was honorably discharged for tuberculosis between 27 and 29 January. A search of WWI draft registration records reveals an entry for a Carl Marion Atherton. He registered twice—once in Idaho Falls, Idaho, on 5 June 1917, and indicated that he was 17 years old—too young to serve. The second registration, in San Francisco, California, is undated, but says he was 23 years old. This suggests that the second registration took place after 10 September, when he had passed another birthday. But this is a remarkable discovery in that the reverse side identifies the date of Carl's discharge, January 28, and his infantry unit, the 20th Infantry. The 20th Infantry was one of the regiments assigned to Fort Douglas.

In September 1919, Carl Marion Atherton applied for a job with the Northern Pacific Railway and denied any physical ailment that might render him unfit for railroad service. He was still working for the railroad well into the 1960s and living in Covina, Los Angeles, California. A Find-A-Grave.com entry for Carl Marion Atherton indicated that he was born on 10 September 1897 in Missouri, and died in Los Angeles County on 4 November 1985. If this is Anna's friend Carl Atherton, he certainly outlived his tuberculosis.

Carl Atherton's WWI draft registration card with discharge information.

Wednesday, 30 January 1918—Weather:

Lunched with Viv. & Bert. Carl & Mr. Rowe came down and we all went to the Orpheum and the Palace after. The show was good and one comedian was so funny I shall never forget him. He had a cute bow[18].

Orpheum Vaudeville Program, *Salt Lake Tribune*, 30 January 1918, page 11.

It is difficult to be certain about where Anna and all her friends went after the show at the Orpheum. A number of downtown places bore the name *Palace*, but a pretty good guess might be the Palace Confectionary on Main Street. It's probably safe to say they didn't go to the Palace Laundry.

Thursday, 31 January 1918—Weather:

Nothing exciting happened. Sewed in evening. I was extremely surprised by a letter from Mr. Clearence Peterson[19] who is in Ogden. He wishes to become better a[c]quainted if not in person by writing.

2

FEBRUARY
AN EARLY SPRING BUT NO PEACE

Friday, 1 February 1918—Weather:

Mother & I sat up and sewed on Miss [Adelaide] Byertine's dress until one A.M. It is very pretty. Laura thinks she has the mumps[20].

Sometime during February and March, the unit to which Oswin Rands was attached was reduced to a "training cadre" and sent to Saint-Aignan-des-Noyers in central France, where "systematic training" was begun. Saint-Aignan is a sparsely populated rural place in the Loire Valley, very remote.

Saturday, 2 February 1918—Weather:

Purchased a new pair of dark brown military-heeled shoes. Rushed home and finished afore said dress.

Brown military-heeled style shoes popular in the 1920s.

Sunday, 3 February 1918—Weather:

I did not go to S.S. But to a funeral instead. Bro. Picket's little girl's [funeral]. Le & Ruby & baby blessed[21]. We were down there for a delightful dinner. Mr. Clever phoned to me while I was away.

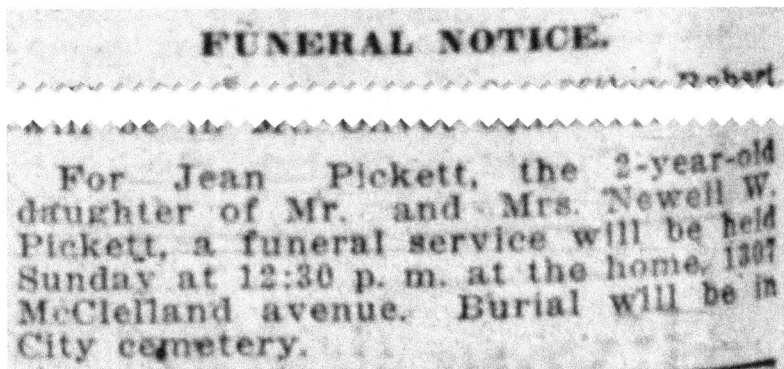

FUNERAL NOTICE.

For Jean Pickett, the 2-year-old daughter of Mr. and Mrs. Newell W. Pickett, a funeral service will be held Sunday at 12:30 p. m. at the home, 1307 McClelland avenue. Burial will be in City cemetery.

The funeral notice for 2 year-old Jean Pickett who died from bronchopneumonia, *Deseret News*, 1 February 1918, page 2.

The Funeral Notice for Jean Pickett, the daughter of Newell and Stella Pickett, indicates that the funeral was held on February 3 at their home at 1307 McClelland Avenue, located about five blocks from the Lund home. It is likely that the Picketts were members of the same church congregation. Jean's death certificate indicates she died from bronchopneumonia.

Monday, 4 February 1918—Weather: Beautiful & Spring like.

Lunched with Bert & Isabell Steward & Vivian. A letter came from John also from the camp Hospital. Guess I'll go to school again tonight. I met Sergt. Martin.

Although the details of the following notice are absent, it may be a sign of the beginning of an ominous problem.

Hospital Overflowing.

The county hospital being crowded to its capacity it has become necessary to make accommodations for several cases outside of the institution. One case was treated yesterday at the city hospital. There are now more than 100 patients in the county institution.

Signs of impending growth in hospital overcrowding, *Deseret News*, 4 February 1918, page 14.

Tuesday, 5 February 1918—Weather:

Went out and purchased a new Spring hat. But I won't wear it until later in the season. Went to mutual[22] in evening. Attended a "dime dance" after. Had a fairly good time. Today was more like Spring than ever.

> A "dime dance," often called a "taxi dance," was a social dance where young men would purchase dance tickets at the door for 10 cents each. When they wanted to dance with a girl for one song, they would give her a ticket. Usually at the end of the evening, the girl could redeem her tickets for a commission. This event could have been a church social mixer or a fund raiser for the war effort.

Wednesday 6 February 1918—Weather: Cloudy & Spring like.

A chill wind is blowing but still it seems like Spring. To school in evening. As I was waiting for my car to come home, the report came out that the SS *Tuscania*[23] was sunk off the coast of Ireland. I think I cried all the way home. Over 2,000 boys were sent to Davy Jone's Locker. Letter from Mr. Mead.

The troop ship SS *Tuscania* torpedoed and sunk off the coast of Ireland, *The New York Times*, 7 February 1918, page 1.

Anna's remark about "waiting for [her] car" is the first time she gives a hint about how she traveled between home, work, and elsewhere so readily. A search at the main library at Salt Lake City indicated that in 1918 the city had a light rail system run by the Utah Light and Traction Co., which would have afforded easy access to most of the city, including Fort Douglas.

The word *traction* in the name of the owner of the street car line derives from the difficulty that the early street car developers had in getting their experimental cars to have sufficient traction on the rails going over bumps and hills in the city during icy weather. The company with the most reliable traction was the company that stood to gain the most from electrified street cars — the company that supplied the streetlights. Hence, the Utah Light and Traction Co.

Waiting for the Trolley Car on Main Street, 12 May 1918, where Anna would have stood every weekday on her way home.

The war had a curious impact on a practical aspect of riding on Salt Lake City's street cars. The addition of a one- or two-cent war tax on so many commodities and services made it convenient for people to save pennies when otherwise they might have discarded them or passed them on to their children's piggy banks. Furthermore, the local government issued special coins to cover the lack of U.S. pennies.

Haughty Conductors Must Take Pennies On Street Cars

WAR pennies, the kind that have been flooding the penny-less West since the inauguration of war taxes, extra penny charges and the other litle incidentals of the war, are legal tender on street cars, despite the protestations of penny-laden conductors.

That is the edict that went forth today from the offices of H. F. Dicke, general manager of the Utah Light and Traction company.

Patrons of the company have complained of late that conductors have refused to accept pennies in payment for fares.

Probably never before have pennies been so plentiful in the West as since the beginning of the war, according to Mr. Dicke, and where Westerners were in the habit of throwing pennies away they now save them.

This brought about the unprecedented condition of having five pennies offered for street car fares, and conductors have been loath to accept them.

To compel the conductors' to accept pennies for fares, Mr. Dicke this morning issued a bulletin ordering all conductors to accept without comment all pennies that are offered for fares.

Street car conductors required to accept pennies for war-time fares, *Salt Lake Telegram*, 1 January 1918, page 2

Thursday, 7 February 1918—Weather: (see below)

Thank God there were only about 150 soldiers lost. We don't know who as yet. My heart is soar for the dear ones who will grieve their death. Who know but that Billy Boy[24] is among them. My eyes fill with hot tears when I allow myself to think of it. It is snowing hard again.

Actually, 230 were lost; of them, 201 were American soldiers.

Friday, 8 February 1918—Weather:

I had my first experience in ass[is]ting the Dr. in an opperation. I had to help set a broken jaw. The physical strain was quite hard and I nearly fainted. Went to school and stayed untill 8:30. I wonder where Billy is. Letter from Sergent John.

Saturday, 9 February 1918—Weather:

Spent noon hr. visiting Vivian. Went to Bonneville Park in evening with Laura. Had a fairly good time.

Sunday, 10 February 1918—Weather:

To S.S. as per usual. Bert came over. Also dady's friend Mr. Geo. Paul & Mr. Brimsike. They dined with us and also spent evening. Mr. Paul told some of his most unusual experiences in S. America. Had a most delightful evening.

Monday, 11 February 1918—Weather:

To school again. After a movie with Viv. Bill is safe, thanks to God. He was not on the *Tuscania* but is in N.Y.

Tuesday, 12 February 1918—Weather:

This is Lincoln's Day, but I am at work as usual. Went home and sewed until 2 A.M. on Mrs. Palmer's dress.

Wednesday, 13 February 1918—Weather

Daddy took Laura and I to a Postal [employees] Ball at the Odeon[25]. Had a nice time. We could hardly get away from Mr. Jack Moore & Mr. Cowel.

The Postal Ball appears to be a significant event throughout the state, and Anna's father, a longtime mail carrier, would have wanted to participate.

Postal Ball Tonight.

With music from a stringed orchestra of 14 pieces and refreshments prepared for over 500 persons, the seventh annual ball of the postal employees, to be held at the Odeon tonight, promises to exceed any previous dance of the association. Richard Gerrans, chairman of the committee who has charge of the program, has received word to prepare for a large attendance from Ogden, Provo and other cities.

The annual post office employees' ball was a significant event in 1918, *Deseret News*, 13 February 1918, page 7.

Thursday, 14 February 1918—Weather:

Home and to bed early. Letter from John.

Friday, 15 February 1918—Weather:

To school after a movie with Viv. Violet[26] took leading part in a Religion class theatrical production. The folks all attended but me. I received a letter from Clarence Peterson. Vernon Castle[27] the famous dancer and airman is killed [while] flying. He was very daring.

Saturday, 16 February 1918—Weather:

Went to show and supper with Viv & Bert. That's all. Mr. Rowe called for me but I wasn't home. I like him just dandy. I wish he would call again.

Sunday, 17 February 1918—Weather:

Stayed home all afternoon; went walking in evening with Viv. Le and Ruby were home for dinner.

Monday, 18 February 1918—Weather:

Went to school as per usual. When I returned home a letter was there from the Sergeant.

Tuesday, 19 February 1918—Weather:

Home immediatly after work. Made a service flag to wear on my sleeve.

A service flag with one star signifying one family member serving in the military.

The Service flag was first displayed in the front windows of homes during WWI to signify a son or husband serving in the Armed Forces. The Lund family would have been entitled to display a service flag with one blue star because Anna's older brother, William, was serving in the Navy. Additional stars were added for multiple family members serving. Businesses were entitled to fly a Service Flag in front of their building with a star for each employee serving in the military.

The Mountain States Telephone and Telegraph Co. building with its many-starred service flag.

Wednesday, 20 February 1918—Weather:

Went to school then to Wasatch Ward carnival after. Had a nice time and tumbled in bed at about 12:30 A.M.

WASATCH WARD TO MAKE MERRY

Four-Day Carnival With Many Attractions Will Be Held at Chapel.

A neighboring church congregation held a four-day carnival to raise funds for a new chapel, *Salt Lake Herald-Republican*, 17 February 1918, page 33.

Thursday, 21 February 1918—Weather

Home early after a movie with the girls.

Friday, 22 February 1918—Weather

This is Washington's Birthday. No work today. Hooray. Sewed on Vivian Kuhn's dress. Went to Ward reunion in evening with folks. Had a nice time. Had one dance. "Grand time."

> **Emerson Ward Reunion**—The bishopric of Emerson ward invite all members of the ward over 16 years of age to attend the annual ward reunion which will be held in the amusement hall on Washington's birthday at 8 o'clock a good program will be rendered, there will be dancing and refreshments will be served.

Anna's church congregation held an annual reunion for all adult members, *Deseret News*, 21 February 1918, page 2.

Saturday, 23 February 1918—Weather:

Back to work again. I saw Mr. Paul and Mr. Brinnicke.

Sunday, 24 February 1818—Weather: [see below]

Snow, rain and sleet all afternoon and evening. Laura & I went to town on a wild goose chase. We were all heate[d] up. Came home and ate dinner at six and we wrote letters.

Monday, 25 February 1918—Weather:

Another letter and three pictures from John. One of them is a regular dream. Sveltest uniform. I went to school as per usual. I placed advertizement cards at the Soldier's Club[28] and at the Fort for a dance in the Ward Friday [see entry for March 1].

Tuesday, 26 February 1918—Weather:

Went home early and worked on Vivian Kuhn's dress. It is Alice blue satin trimed with rose and crystal beads. There are about a dozen soldiers who parade about town in an auto truck and colors flying and band playing. Trying to get recruits. Wish I could be one.

BIG SPRING DRIVE
FOR PATRIOTS IS ON

Salt Lake Army Recruiting Officers Will Conduct Vigorous Campaign.

not already in uniform.

The first step of the big drive came today, when the full Twentieth infantry band of Ft. Douglas made its appearance on the streets to help stimulate recruiting.

The following bulletin calling upon

Ongoing Army recruiting drive with the 20th Infantry Band appearing on the streets of Salt Lake City, *Salt Lake Telegram*, 27 February 1918, page 9.

Wednesday 27 February 1918—Weather:

A letter again this A.M., a dandy too. The band is playing again.

Thursday, 28 February 1918—Weather:

Sewed on Vivian Kuhn's dress until 12 P.M. I received a letter from Douglas Edwards. I wrote an immense letter to John.

It is likely that Douglas Edwards was Anna's first cousin through her mother's father, William Edward Partington. He served in the 62nd Infantry, which was assigned to training at Camp Fremont, near Palo Alto, California.

3

MARCH
SAMMIES AND MAC

Friday, 1 March 1918—Weather: [see below]

It surely seems like Spring is here today. Even the public drinking fountains are running. Went to Character ball in Ward, as Red Cross Nurse. Had grand time. Daddy was Captain Katzengammer. He surely was funny. Mr. Larson & Allan were there from Ft. Douglas.

The Katzenjammer Kids was an American comic strip created by the German immigrant Rudolph Dirks and drawn by Harold H. Knerr for 37 years (1912 to 1949). It debuted 12 December 1897 in *American Humorist*, the Sunday supplement of William Randolph Hearst's *New York Journal*. Dirks was the first cartoonist to express dialogue in comic characters through speech balloons. The Captain, a shipwrecked sailor who later was added to the strip, acted as a surrogate father. For a time, two competing versions of the strip ran concurrently.

The two different renderings of the Captain.

Saturday, 2 March 1918—Weather:

Nothing much doing. Mother was sick when I returned home. I was invited to a house party to Lunstrums with Laura but declined it on account of need of sleep and mother.

Sunday, 3 March 1918—Weather: [see below]

Went to Sabbath School. Stayed home remainder of day. Mother did not rise until 4 P.M. I trimmed my new Spring hat, But the weather is a bit cold for straw as yet. It is grey straw trimmed with green ribbon and assorted cherries.

A straw spring hat trimmed with green ribbon, perhaps similar to Anna's hat.

Monday, 4. March 1918—Weather:

Went to school and took most of my first examination. It was very easy and I hope it will bring me a good mark.

Tuesday, 5 March 1918—Weather:

Went home and made a poster for advertizing Ward Dance at Soldier's club.

The division Oswin Rands belonged to was redesignated as

the Depot Division for the I Corps, or a unit that was to provide replacements for other divisions in the I Corps. Being a Depot Division was very unpopular in the Army because it meant that buddies from the same home town or region would be separated. Oswin might not have been too disappointed, since his original company already had been dispersed. He was attached to a battalion mostly of men from Minnesota.

Wednesday, 6 March 1918—Weather:

Put up afore said poster and went to school. I finished my test. I do hope I have a good report. Sixteen Sammys[29] have been killed by the Huns, and burried in Fra[n]ce. There are battles every day.

Thursday, 7 March 1918—Weather:

I declined an invitation to a party at Lafont's and went with Viv down to see Le & Ruby. We spent a very delightful evening. Le was drauring some show cards. We met Jim Youngberg. Had quite a long chat with him. He wants us to go out to Bingham and visit the mines.

Southwest across the valley from Salt Lake City is a large open-pit copper mine in the Oquirrh Mountains, once known as the Bingham Copper Mine. It has been in production since 1906 and has been a tourist attraction ever since. Today it is known as the *Kennecott Copper Mine.*

The Bingham Copper Mine, ca. 1920.

An ad showing twice daily excursion trains running out to the Bingham Copper Mine and back, *Goodwin's Weekly*, 9 March 1918, page 9.

Friday, 8 March 1918—Weather: (see below)

We are having reel Mar. weather now. I feel hoarse-back-rideish today. Went to school, and my test mark was 97%. Came home early and went to dance with Laura & Grant Helton. I gave him a message for Mac. Now I am sorry I did but it won't hurt.

This is the first mention of Mac. He has not been mentioned by his surname, and from here on out he is just *Mac* or *Mack*. Anna's relationship with Mac began at least nine months earlier and now in the diary is nothing short of enigmatic. In Anna's scrapbook and in her writing fifty years later, several photographs show up referring to a "beau" she labels as McGinnis. She wrote, "[H]e was Irish and a lot of fun. He was much older than I and treated me with the greatest respect" and "he begged me in all sincerity to marry him at Thanksgiving time." She has little good to say about him and claims at one point to discontinue ever seeing him again. Then he shows up again in her life and she willingly allows him court her. The next Sunday morning when he calls and she doesn't want her family to know about it shows her dilemma about how she plans to treat him and how she wants her family to treat him.

Saturday, 9 March 1918—Weather:

Bought some violets and went home. There was a letter from the Sergeant.

Sunday, 10 March 1918—Weather:

Le and Ruby came to dine with us. I had an appointment with Viv. Went down town and saw the fashion show, and a movie. Mac called in the A.M. before S.S. But I won't tell the folks who it was yet for a while for we have been apart for over six months.

Monday, 11 March 1918—Weather:

Mac met me after work and took me to dinner. I then went to school and he escorted me home after. He is the same old boy. Has not changed a bit. I think I heard him call me "Dear" once. He must have forgotten himself. I hope he [doesn't] feel that way about me.

Tuesday, 12 March 1918—Weather:

As I was leaving the office Mac met me and went to the [trolley] car with me. Vivian introduced to me over the phone, Mr. Frank Collins. He invited me out but I refused as I have never seen him.

Wednesday, 13 March 1918—Weather:

Spent noon hr. trying to play pool with Mac at the Army Club. To school as usual. A letter from Clarence.

Thursday, 14 March 1918—Weather:

Spent noon hr trying to [buy] a pair of white gloves. Finally got them. Evening, I went with Mac to the Red Cross Bennefit concert by John McCormack; Irish tenor. The music was wonderful. Over 7,000 people attended. It was held in the Tabernacle[30].

The interior of the Salt Lake Tabernacle filled to capacity.

O wonder John McCormack sang in such splendid spirit the other evening: the tremendous crowd that had assembled in the Tabernacle — some eight thousand in all—was an extraordinary inspiration in itself. The concert was a great success in every way. Salt Lake turned out the largest audience that has greeted the great tenor anywhere along the line; the admissions approximated $10,000—the record receipts for any one performance; McCormack was in fine fettle himself and sang as we have never heard him sing before.

A glowing review of the Red Cross concert held in the Salt Lake City Tabernacle, *Goodwin's Weekly*, 14 March 1918, page 10.

The 107th Ammunition Train was then in training at Coetquidan, France, a French military school that had been turned over to the American Expeditionary Force for training purposes. It was located in Brittany, northwestern France. This is based on *United States Army in the World War, 1917-1919, Training and Use of American Units with the British and French*, Volume 3, p. 647.

Friday, 15 March 1918—Weather:

Went to school then met Mac & Laura and then to character dance at 11th Ward (church meeting house). Had a nice time. I represented a Red Cross nurse & Laura, "Spring."

Saturday, 16 March 1918—Weather:

Nothing much doing. I met Marva Spencer at Walker's[31]. Gee, but I like her. I hope I can know her better. I went home and to bed early.

Sunday, 17 March 1918—Weather:

After Sabbath I sewed all afternoon. Mr. Rowe & Mr. Morgan of the 20th Infantry came & spent the evening. They are both dandy boys. I believe I want them to come again. Evelyn Paramore told me about her romance. Bert & Viv called too.

Monday, March 18, 1918—Weather:

Went to school after seeing Mary Pickford at the Paramont[32]. It was the best I have ever seen her play. I came home early as I was not feeling in the pink of condition.

Mary Pickford at the Paramount Theater, *Salt Lake Tribune*, 18 March 1918, page 9.

Tuesday ,19 March 1918—Weather:

Went up to the Capitol Building for Dr. Tripp. I also discovered during my noon hour that, as I had suspected, Mac has tried to fool me again. I think I shall try a little of his own medicine on him. Viv & Bert came over for a few minutes in the P.M. Viv tried on her dress.

Wednesday, 20 March 1918—Weather:

Salt Lake has been badly fooled by a fake Indian Chief & Princess[33]. They collected money and had a public marriage. The Mayor even kissed her. Now they have skipped. Good joke. Now the evening paper claims different. I should worry. Went out with Mac in P.M.

Thursday, 21 March 1918—Weather:

Hurried home and sewed on Viv's dress besides washing and ironing a few things for myself.

Friday, 22 March 1918—Weather: Weather just like summer.

Mac met me at noon. We had a game of pool and then I found information regarding the lots next door west. Went to supper with Mac & then after school we wandered around a little then came home. We had one hillarious time. We both felt gay.

Saturday, 23 March 1918—Weather:

I went out and purchased some violets. After work went with Viv up to her aunt's home who is quarentined for Scarlet Fever. I was so tired when I got home. Went to bed early.

The City Board of Health posted a bulletin that day stating that communicable and infectious diseases were up slightly from previous weeks. Anna's cavalier attitude about visiting a home with someone quarantined with an infectious disease is curious.

The report shows a slight increase in the number of contagious diseases reported. Smallpox has increased again and whooping cough has spread. There were 265 cases of contagious and infectious diseases reported, as follows:

Mumps, 57; chickenpox, 53; whooping cough, 40; German measles, 36; smallpox, 27; measles, 27; scarlet fever, 18; diphtheria, 5; meningitis, 1 and typhoid fever 1.

City Board of Health Report of increased number of communicable diseases, *Salt Lake Telegram*, 23 March 1918, page 2.

Sunday, 24 March 1918—Weather:

To Sunday S. as usual. I sewed all day. Layed off long enough to run over to Wilson's for a minute. I met Gotleib Lindow's wife with others. I have two dresses to make this week at nights.

On 7 January 1918, James Gotlieb Lindow married Lilian Leona Alred. He was 21 years old and was from Illinois and she was 16 years old and was from Salk Lake City. In the 1920 U.S. Census, the individuals residing at 1206 Bryan Avenue include some Lindows as well as Wilsons. Anna's comment can be interpreted to mean that she met Gotleib Lindow's wife, Lilian, while she was visiting the Wilsons.

Monday, 25 March 1918—Weather:

Hurried home and sewed all evening. Laura heard from Lang. I don't hear from John any more. I guess he has another. Well there are plenty more. Bert suddenly went under an operation for penticitus[34]. She is getting on dandy. Poor kid it is the only way she will ever get rest.

Tuesday, 26 March 1918—Weather:

I went to see her today at noon. Mrs. Byerline came in evening and fitted her dress. The Germans are making their Spring drive now[35]. I only wish it was only a horrible nightmare. But we must keep up our spirits.

Wednesday, 27 March 1918—Weather: Rained all day steadily.

Went shopping at noon with Viv. In evening I sewed until 12 again. The Germans are being repulsed again. Their man loss is estimated at 400,000 & the British loss at 100,000. Isn't it horrible.

Thursday, 28 March 1918—Weather: Fair and chilly.

Mac & I went out to see Bert at the hospital and lunched at Drewel & Travkey. Home again to sew all night again.

Friday, 29 March 1918—Weather: Beautiful fair & warm.

Mac met me again and we played pool. Perhaps someday I shall know how. Bert has pnewmonia now. Poor kid! Mother just phoned that a letter came from France. I hope it is from John. It will make me so happy. It was from Oswin Rands, an old time would be sweet heart. Tho I was glad to hear from him, I was disappointed. Vivian came in P.M.

Aha! Here it is. Anna finally mentions her future husband, my grandfather—"an old time would be sweet heart." I have little clue as to when and how they met. Oh, how I wish we had a copy of this letter! It is probably safe to say they met before 1918, perhaps when Anna's family visited her mother's sister's family who were living in Rexburg, Idaho. Ozzie was from Rexburg and did not move to Utah with his family until 1919. Anna married Ozzie in Salt Lake City on 17 March 1921.

Saturday, 30 March 1918—Weather:

I have gotten rid of Mrs. Byerline's dress at last. Sat up till 1:45 A.M. working on Viv's dress. I received a...

Anna left this entry incomplete. Perhaps it was a letter that left her speechless.

Sunday, 31 March 1918—Weather: Warm & Sunny.

Sewed on Viv's dress in A.M. Sent it home. Fixed my own clothes a little & went on a ten-mile hike with Mac at 4:40 P.M. Came home about 9:15 by Summer time. Le & Ruby were at the house. This day marks the first day of Summer time or in other words, all clocks are advance one hour till Sept. A very pleasant Easter.

The Original acts of Congress establishing Summer Time, or Daylight Savings Time (DST) in the United States. It took a war to make it happen.

Starting on 30 April 1916, three years earlier, Germany and its World War I allies (Austria-Hungary) were the first to use Daylight Savings Time (DST; German: *Sommerzeit*) as a way to conserve coal during wartime. Britain, most of its allies, and many European neutrals soon followed suit. Russia and a few other countries waited until the next year, and the United States adopted it in 1918 and set summer DST to begin on 31 March 1918.

On the day of Anna's hike with Mac, sunset would have taken place at 6:50 P.M. When they arrived at home about 9:15 DST, it would have been 8:15 P.M. standard time, or about 10 minutes before twilight ended at 8:23 P.M.[36]

4

APRIL
'I Love My Freedom More'

Monday, 1 April 1918 DST—Weather: [see below]

This is a beautiful day and I feel fineree. I went to the houspital to see Bert with Viv. She looks better than ever before. Went to school in evening. Was tired. Left at eight.

Tuesday, 2 April 1918—Weather: [see below]

It has snowed all day and is cold as the dickens. I went to see Bert. I took some magazines to the sick people at the hospital. Wrote a regastered letter to Robert Mead at Camp Dodge[37]. The others didn't reach him. Perhaps this one will. Viv quit her job. Went home and to bed at 9:30. I guess the Seargent is married.

Wednesday, 3 April 1918—Weather: Cold and cloudy all day.

Went to school, but had dinner with Mack before. Then he and I went out to Ruby's & Le's home and had a dandy time. We walked home.

Thursday, 4 April 1918—Weather:

I received a letter from John announcing his marriage. I hope he is happy. Evidently he is. Bert is home now. I visited her. She looks fine.

Friday, 5 April 1918—Weather: Fair & chilly.

I mailed a silver sea shell as a wedding gift and wrote a congratulatory letter to John. To think that had I only cared I might have been the dear girl. Went to school. I met Sergt. Marten. Chatted for a few minutes. Vivian called.

Saturday, 6 April 1918—Weather: Fair & Warmer.

There are a great many conference visitors[38]. This is the first anaversery of U.S. entering the War. The third Liberty Loan drive has begun[39]. I have purchased materiel for my coat. Met Mable L. & Evelyn Paramore. Also saw Winn.

Sunday, 7 April 1918—Weather: Clowdy and a little rain.

Laura & I went to ten o'clock conference in the Tabernacle. Went to see Bert after. Gee but my foot was sore. I could hardly navigate. Went home and sewed on my coat all afternoon and evening. I wish something exciting would happen right away.

Monday, 8 April 1918—Weather: Warm and sunny.

Went to school again as per usual, only I was late as I went home & dressed for a dance first. Mac and Laura met me at nine and to the Eagles hall[40] we went to Dr. H. B. Sprague's Ambulence Benefit. The best dance I have ever attended. We all had a wonderful evening. I had as high as six invitations for a dance. "Some big time" I could have danced for a week.

It sure would be interesting to know what Anna's criteria was for a "big time" dance partner. Especially when her big-time suitor, Mac, was with her.

Announcement for Sprague's Ambulance Benefit Dance at Eagles' Hall,
Salt Lake Herald-Republican, 7 April 1918, page 19.

Tuesday 9 April 1918—Weather: Fair & warmer.

Played pool with Mac at noon. went to officers & teachers meeting[41]. A
very good lecture was given by Conway Ashton. I packed John's pictures
up and back they go. All that soft[42] stuff written will now be ment for wify.

Wednesday, 10 April 1918—Weather:

I have been out to lunch. I visited Winnie & Marva Spencer. Now it is
thunderin. Guess it'll rain. Mac phoned this A.M. Went to school at 5:20.
Left at 8 and visited Viv & Bert. The Allies are having a fierce struggle. The
Huns are holding their own and then some.

Thursday, 11 April 1918—Weather:

Sewed on my coat. Vivian Kuhn was visiting us. Mack phoned. Viv & Bert
also visited for a little while.

The 41st Division began to function as the replacement division
for the entire American Expeditionary Force, not just the I Corps.

Many units of the division were transferred to the 32nd Division. Since Oswin Rands was listed as part of the 32nd Division, the 57th Field Artillery Battalion, and the 107th Ammunition Train in June and upon his return at the end of the war, I assume that it was during this period when he was transferred.

Friday, 12 April 1918—Weather:

Went to school at 5:30. Met Mack at 7:30 and went out to the first preseason dance[43]. Le & Ruby were there. We also met a few other people we know. There were thousands out there. Mack still says I am the "Girl of Girls." The Germans have gained more growrnd, the last few days[44].

PRESEASON DANCE AT SALTAIR TOMORROW

R. Owen Sweeten and his band of twenty-four pieces are daily rehearsing the new dance music which Director Sweeten has been collecting in anticipation of the preseason dances which open at Saltair tomorrow night. it is stated by the management of the resort that the big pavilion has been thoroughly renovated and the floor again put in the first-class condition for which it is famed.

The first train for the resort leaves at 7:45 p. m. tomorrow and immediately on its arrival dancing will commence. The second train will leave the saltair depot at 8:15. The same train fare as heretofore will apply to these preseason dances, and each Friday and Tuesday evening will see the immense pavilion lighted until the formal opening of Saltair Decoration day.

Ample preparations have been made to handle the big crowds that are expected on the opening night.

Announcement for the first preseason dance at the Saltair Resort, *Salt Lake Herald-Republican*, 11 April 1918, page 4.

Saturday, 13 April 1918—Weather:

Home and to bed.

Sunday, 14 April 1918—Weather:

The church in A.M. I sewed all afternoon. Le & Ruby came. Mac went to church with me. After, Le & Ruby & Mac & I went walking. Got back at 10:30 and Joan & her hubby were there. Had a pleasant evening. Mac wouldn't hardly go. He wants me to get married as per usual. But nothing doing.

Monday, 15 April 1918—Weather: Snowed all fornoon.

Mack came and took me to dinner. He says he has it all figured out. A house all ready and a lot more things. He wishes my answer tomorrow. It is so funny I have to laugh. Is very selfish of me but I love my freedom more. Guess I'll go to school again. Letter from Mead. To dance with Laura & Helton. Dandy time.

Tuesday, 16 April 1918—Weather: Fair and cold.

Nothing much doing today. Mead said that he's doing guard duty in N.W. and that over 40,000 men left for "Over There" last week. Mack & Helton took Laura & I out to Saltair[45]. We had a dandy time. We changed escorts at last. This is my 20th birthday. Mack gave me a 10 lb. box of chocolates. Mother & Lal. (Laura Andrea Lund) a g[e]orgette waist[46] & a potted flower [birthday gifts]. Held check.

Anna's twentieth birthday photo found in her scrapbook.

The Saltair Amusement Resort on the shores of the Great Salt Lake.

Wednesday, 17 April 1918—Weather: Cold.

Laura & I spent our noon hour sleeping in the Y.W.C.A. rooms. I went to school. Hurried home to get some sleep and could not after all for Lewis Grossen and Mr. Senior called and spent the evening with the excuse of selling W.S. [War Savings] Bonds. A very nice evening anyhow.

Thursday, 18 April 1819—Weather:

I was surprised to see Mack waiting for me at noon. He brought Laura's book back to her. We went to dinner at Young's Cafe[47]. Best place in town. Good looking waiters too. Home and sewed all evening.

Friday, 19 April 1918—Weather:

Spent my noon roaming around with Evelyn Paramore Radabaugh[48]. She is very sorry that she married when she did. I would be too. Went to school and Mack and Laura met me after. We first went to the Eagles Hall then to the Odeon. Had a nice time at the latter.

It is amazing how Anna seems to know where every dance is happening that is open to the public.

Saturday, 20 April 1918—Weather:

Accidentally met Mack at noon. I also met Evelyne again. I went right home and sewed a little. Laura went to the Odeon.

Sunday, 21 April 1918—Weather: Sunny & warmer.

I did not go to S.S. but remained at home and finished my coat. It looks fine. Navy blue wool crepe with ivory buttons & buckles. Mack came at 6:30 and we visited with Viv & Bert. Now tonight I like him fine and sometimes I just hate him.

Monday, 22 April 1918—Weather: [see below]

Met Marva Spencer and then Laura. Now we are having summer again. Evelyne came down and had her dress fitted. Viv & Bert called in the office.

COUNTY OFFICES TO CLOSE LIBERTY DAY

All county offices will close at noon next Friday, in observance of Liberty day. The proclamation issued by President Wilson last week setting Friday, April 26, apart as a national holiday for the observance of the one hundred and forty-second anniversary of American independence, was read at the county commission meeting this morning by Chairman C. F. Stillman. The commission voted unanimously to give a half holiday to all county employes.

The announcement that Liberty Day would be celebrated with half-day off on Friday, *Salt Lake Telegram*, 22 April 1918, page 2.

Tuesday, 23 April 1918—Weather: Beautiful Day also ideal Moon.

Went out to Saltair with Mack & Le & Ruby. Had a nice time. Mack and I growled at one another all evening. Then at last when we got home he started proposing again. He says the house is all ready for us to go to, but nothing doing.

Wednesday, 24 April 1918—Weather: Lovely day.

Went to movies in evening with Viv & Bert. Sewed when returned home & Viv & Bert came over.

Thursday, 25 April 1918—Weather: Clowdy but pleasant.

I went walking at noon with Mack. He surely is a lot of fun. Hurried home early to sew, which I did till about ten o'clock. I received a letter from Clearance Peterson in Logan.

Friday, 26 April 1918—Weather:

This is Liberty Day. I asked for a raise. I attended a big Red Cross rally at the Tabernacle. It was a wonderful sight. There were at least 1,500 women in white costume and four companies of soldiers seated in the center and front and the rest of the hall packed with civilians. Music & speaches were given. A British hero soldier spoke enthusiastically.

Liberty Day was proclaimed by the President of the United States (Woodrow Wilson) and generally observed in every state. The purpose was to stimulate the sale of the Third Liberty Loan Issue. Actually, President Wilson's original proclamation did not specify that it was to be a national holiday, and Utah's governor did not want people to take the day off. He exhorted everyone to work harder to help bring the war to an end. But little by little, the day became more like a holiday, until Washington exhorted every state to declare it a legal holiday. The celebration in Salt Lake City was expected to overflow the city's largest assembly hall, the Tabernacle.

Utah's allotment was $10,315,000, and the sales to 77,000 subscribers totaled in round numbers $12,500,000 (as reported in the *Improvement Era*, June 1918, p. 750, the principal Mormon magazine, known today as *The Liahona*.

LIBERTY DAY TO BE OBSERVED BY ALL THE STATES

Patriotic   Demonstrations
Planned in Almost Every
City and Town From
Atlantic to Pacific.

WASHINGTON WILL HAVE BIG PARADE

Acknowledgement that Liberty Day would be a national holiday, expected to raise $2 trillion, *Salt Lake Tribune*, 26 April 1918, page 8.

Saturday, 27 April 1918—Weather: Beautiful day.

Sewed all evening. I got a raise in salary.

Sunday, 28 April 1918—Weather:

I sewed until 2 P.M. Mack took me to the ball game[49]. After which we went to Parker's store[50]. Mrs. Parker is just dandy. Walked through the park and met Laura, Kate & Vivian K. Came home. Had a lot of fun. Ate lunch then Mr. Morgan & Ruth R came. We sang songs then Mack & I walked with Kate. I shall never see him again. Sad but true.

Monday, 29 April 1918—Weather: Summery today.

Had my teeth examined by Dr. Ramsey[51]. Sewed all evening again. We received a letter from Billy and we cannot know his whereabouts[52]. Anyhow we know he is well.

The USS *Pittsburgh*, a WWI armored cruiser famous for the first fixed-wing aircraft landing on a warship, in San Francisco Bay on 18 January 1911.

Tuesday, 30 April 1918—Weather:

I went out to Le's place and ordered some dry goods. I accidentally or perhaps purposely (who knows) met Mack. He is in trouble. He always comes to me with them. Later I talked with a Miss Birch. That was sufficient. I hope I shall never see or [hear] from him again. He is the lowest vilest creature existing & most deceitful. I shall try to forget. At any rate I have learned a good deal.

Wow! What an assertion about a man whom Anna had so much fun with. We don't know how long she was acquainted with him, and it would be fascinating to discover who he was and what he did that caused Anna to be so upset with him.

5

MAY

Tulips and Machines

Wednesday, 1 May 1918—Weather:

I got violet's pictures today. They were pretty good. Vivian K. & Kate Drot also Ruth R & a Mr. Chapman & friend called. Had a funny evening. Kate won Mr. Chap[man's] heart.

Thursday, 2 May 1918—Weather:

I have finished Evelyn's dress at *last*. Home again to sew on my waist.

Friday, 3 May 1918—Weather:

I rushed home and started on my white silk Middy. Which I think very pretty.

Middy blouses were popular sailor-style blouses of the time, sometimes called *waists*.

Saturday, 4 May 1918—Weather:

Mac met me after work and I shall never see him again. I told him I hated him & not to touch me. He has been so deceitful & taken advantage of my kindness to him. I visited Viv & Bert at nine in P.M.

Sunday, 5 May 1918—Weather:

Went to Sunday School & Fast meeting[53]. Vivian & Kate came & we all went to the First Ward[54] then Kate left & we visited Winche's. We had a delightful evening.

Monday, 6 May 1918—Weather:

I went to school for the first time in two weeks. It was fine to get back. I love to study anyhow. I took my white shoes back & received a credit slip.

Tuesday, 7 May 1918—Weather:

Spent noon with Laura & Evelye P. I spent an hour with my typwritter[55] at school. A Card came from Billy. He is in Rio de Janeiro, Argentina[56].

Woman with an Underwood typewriter, ca. 1918

Wednesday, 8 May 1918—Weather:

Doctor is out of town today. The office is getting a good cleaning. I went home for awhile. I then after 5 P.M. went to a movie with Viv. Then to school. I did not have my short ha[n]d at all.

Thursday, 9 May 1918—Weather: It's raining all day.

I spent my noon wandering with Laura in the rain. Attended a gift shower on Evelyne P. Radabaugh. Had a nice time but there wasn't much of a shower. Laura & I gave her a heavy bath towel.

Friday, 10 May 1918—Weather:

I received some motherly advise from an old school friend who was Sarah Larson. She is surely a married stiff. Not for mine though. Went to school again. I got angry at the teacher. I'll chastize her I guess. She surely is a nut of nuts.

Saturday, 11 May 1918—Weather: Swell day again.

I spent my noon hour with Evelyne. Dr. Tripp presented me with over a dozen exclusive tulips for Mother's Day tomorrow. Spent evening tearing around with Ruby. We sure done "some" tearinging too.

Sunday, 12 May 1918—Weather:

Attended Mother's Day services at 10 A.M. Served remainder of day. Le & Ruby came.

Monday, May 13, 1918 - Weather:

I met Evelyne at noon. I saw *Journey's End*[57] at the American. Then went to school. Home early & hit the hay at 11 P.M. A letter came from Robert J. Mead. He is on the East coast.

Tuesday, 14 May 1918—Weather:

Home & sewed in evening. The folks all went to an excellent patriotic rally[58] in the Ward [meeting house]. Gee! I wish something interesting would happen or perhaps come.

Wednesday, 15 May 1918—Weather: Beautiful summer day.

Went shopping. Met Winn & her friend; also Marva Spencer. Attended school then a dance after. Had a punk time.

Thursday, 16 May 1918—Weather:

Saw Mrs. Merrill & visited Viv & Bert. It was Mother's Birthday [her 49th]. Had a nice dinner. Then made my hat and started Viv's.

Friday, 17 May 1918—Weather:

To school as per usual. To bed early. The Germans are slowing down recently. Perhaps in preparation for another big drive. Everything is being made ready for the Second Red Cross War fund drive. $100,000,000 must be raised.

Saturday, 18 May 1918—Weather:

Went shoping with Mother[,] Don & Violet after work. Watched the Moose Heart patriotic parade. Violet & I attended a movie after. A letter & picture came from Clearance Peterson. He is very nice looking.

Moose Red Cross Pageant Plans Ready
Spectacular Parade Moves at 7 Tonight

"SQUIRTEM," the Unusual Moose, which will be feature of the patriotic pageant tonight by the Salt Lake lodge of Moose. Secretary G. C. Hoffman is holding the docile animal.

TRIBUNE STAFF PHOTO

World's Largest Flag to Catch Donations for 'Mercy Organization.'

Moose Red Cross Parade with "Squirtem," the Unusual Moose, *Salt Lake Tribune*, 18 May 1918, page 9.

A significant feature of the parade was 300 women who carried the Moose's 300-foot-long American flag, said to be the largest flag in the country. Spectators were to throw money onto the flag as a donation to the Red Cross.

The Loyal Order of the Moose was founded in 1888 as a white men's social club. A school named Mooseheart was established.

Sunday, 19 May 1918—Weather:

Went to S.S. as usual. Then with Laura to S.S. Union[59] at Stake [Tabernacle] at 2:30. Walked through the Park home. Talked to Mrs. Parker. Mack is in the Guard house for three mos. He said he was going to get desperate and he did. Poor foolish Mack.

Monday, 20 May 1918—Weather:

To school again.

Tuesday, 21 May 1918—Weather:

Not much doing. Big Red Cross parade at 3:30 in which Mother & Laura & I took part wearing white uniforms. A dandy parade. English, French & Belgium heroes were in it and great lines of our own soldiers and flags & banners & bands.

Wednesday, 22 May 1918—Weather:

Same here. Only school.

Thursday, 23 May 1918—Weather:

Home early and sewed. This is Red Cross week and Utah has nearly reached its quota of $500,000. A great campaine is being waged all over the U.S. to raise $100,000,000 for the great mercy work.

Friday, 24 May 1918—Weather:

Spent noon with Laura.

Saturday, 25 May 1918—Weather: Chilly and fair.

Viv & Bert came in and we road home together. Not much doing. I practiced for my speech for S. S.

Sunday, 26 May 1918—Weather:

I gave my speach on Memorial Day and it was a total failure to me, tho others said it was very good. Le & Ruby came. We had some pictures taken. Viv called also. I wrote to Oswin Rands in France & Robt. Mead in New York.

Monday, 27 May 1918—Weather: Very cold towards evening.

Went to school. I was so tired I could sleep anywhere.

Tuesday, 28 May 1918—Weather:

Went to Fort Douglas with Laura & Kate on business. On way home we met two soldier friends and walked through the Park together. Then while they were here [Sherman] & Ed Cederholme called on their machines. I thought at first I was in a pickle. We had to send the last away.

Wednesday, 29 May 1918—Weather: Still cool.

Viv called in. I bought my S.S. Book[60]. The German drive has slowed down some & the Americans have the situation well in hand. Went to canteen work at 7:15 at D & R.G[61]. Served Soldiers. They were dandies. Had a grant time. Then went to Myrtle Palmer's for P.M.

Thursday, 30 May 1918—Weather:

Mother & Dad & the rest of us went to the Orpheum Matenee then to the cemetery. Laura & I strolled in the Park afterwards on our way home. The Germans have broken through a little further on the French and British lines. The Americans have driven them back somewhere else[62].

Orpheum Vaudeville program for week of 25 May 1918.

Friday, 31 May 1918—Weather: Cool and Fair.

I attended the organ recital[63] at the Tabernacle at noon. It was wonderful. I love every spot in the Temple Square. I went to night school and road home with Ellen Hansen.

The pipes of the Tabernacle Organ, a widely recognized Mormon icon, considered one of the largest and finest organs in the world.

6

JUNE
'Of Course I Am Stunning in It'

Saturday, 1 June 1918—Weather: Moderately warm.

Spent noon with Laura & Evelyne. Visited the new community house. Viv & Bert came in the office. Home early and set out aster plants. Mack called and wishes me to see him so he may explain the cause of his lockup. I guess he'll always love me & care. Poor boy.

> In several large Utah cities, new community centers were being constructed in city parks where the nearby residents had access to facilities for reading, music, dancing, dramatics, lectures, swimming, recreation and outdoor movies. One such center was being built at Liberty Park, a favorite place for Anna and her family.

Sunday, 2 June 1918—Weather: Ideal June day. Mosquitos.

Took my new S.S. class for the first time & gave lesson[64]. Visited the military hospital with Marva S. & Ellen Hansen. Met some nice boys and went walking with them. Mr. Rowe came while I was gone but took Laura out. Then later had a heart to heart chat. Viv & Bert came too in P.M.

Monday, 3 June 1918—Weather:

Attended organ recital at tabernacle. It was elegant. Went to school and came home early. Sherman & Ed Cederhorn took Laura & I motor riding. Had a dandy time.

Tuesday, 4 June 1918—Weather: Gee! its Hot.

Spent noon with Laura. I am in love with Mr. Rowe. But he is in love with someone else. Well thats always my luck. Gee! but I think he is grand.

Wednesday, 5 June 1918—Weather: [see below]

Nothing much doing only its as hot as blazes. I wish something exciting would happen. Today is the second registration day for soldiers[65]. Viv & I met Corp. Newton Rains & Privt. Horace Andrews of B Co. 20 Inf[66]. They are some of the nicest "Gentlemen" I have ever met. Viv served lunch.

Thursday, 6 June 1918—Weather:

Spent noon with Vivian Khern. Not much doing. Sewed on my gingham dress. Re'cd a letter from Shirley Stewart of the Coast Artillary[67], whom I met at the [D&RG] on the 29 last. It was surely a nice letter. Was glad to receive it for he has brown eyes and a charming smile.

Friday, 7 June 1918—Weather: Hot as the devil himself. (86°)

Spent noon with Laura & Evelyne. Cousin Joe Evans[68] came to see us. I sluffed school and went to a movie with him. Had a dandy time. He is surely a dandy boy, and so sweet & generous. Tho he is deaf, we understand one another very well. He certainly is a handsome fellow too.

Saturday, 8 June 1918—Weather:

[Quit] work at 1:20. Porky Evans & wife came to see us but Joe & I went to the ball game. Then out to Saltair with Joan & Eddy Evans & their better halfs. We went in the water then for a ride on the launch. Had a grand time. Joe stayed at our house.

Sunday, 9 June 1918—Weather: Boiling hot.

I love my S.S. class work. Went to sleep in afternoon. Then to Park and boat ride with Laura & Joe. Had a nice time. He is charmed by Laura & Laura & I are infatuated with him. Oh I am so tired.

Monday, 10 June 1918—Weather: Hotest day in 18 years[69]. 100°

Went to school but couldn't stand it. Joseph Evans went home this A.M.

Tuesday, 11 June 1918—Weather:

Went to a party with Laura up on B St. Had a nice time, as there was a lot of good ice cream & cake. Walter is in love with Laura.

Wednesday, 12 June 1918—Weather: Hot all the time.

Finished my gingham dress. It sure is pretty. Of course, I am stunning in it. Went out on W. S. S. drive[70]. No success as yet.

Thursday, 13 June 1918—Weather:

Filled out a report of myself for the Red Cross Canteen service. Eddy Evans phoned. Home and at work on Mrs. Byerline's dress. I took my annual shower on the lawn and it was great.

Oswin Rands was transferred to Company A of the 107th Ammunition Train in the 32nd Division, from the Headquarters Company of the 57th Field Artillery Brigade.

Friday, 14 June 1918—Weather: Triffle cooler. Clowdy.

Had Dr. Thomas examine my teeth. He says they are pretty good.

Saturday, 15 June 1918—Weather:

Hurried home after work. Came to town later with Viol to a movie. Tom Saywer & Huckleberry Fin.[71]

Oswin Rands, now assigned to the 107th Ammunition Train in the 32nd Division, was from this date until 22 July 1918 located in Centre, Alsace, France, near the Rhine River south of Strasbourg. The 32nd Division was defending the Belfort Gap during the Vosges Front, which was actually in German territory. See the map that follows.

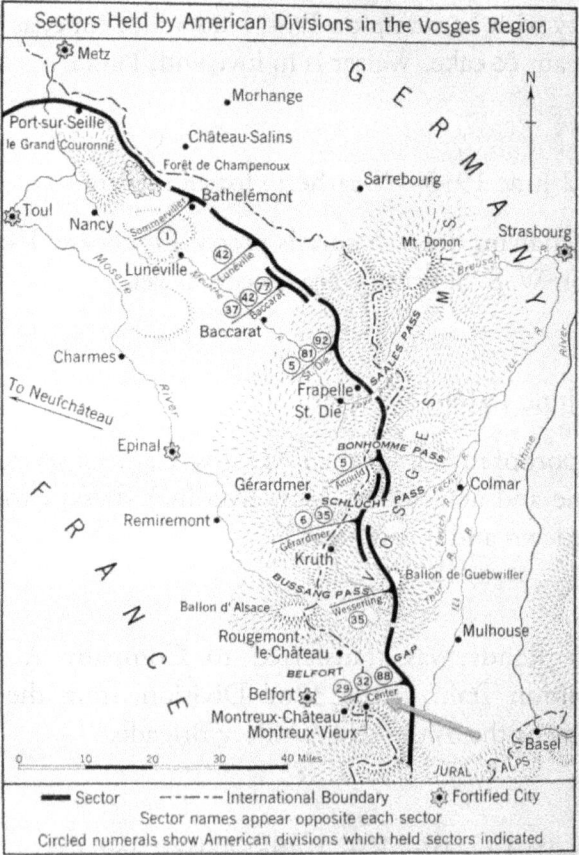

Map showing the location of American troops, including the 32nd Division, during the months of June and July 1918.

Sunday, 16 June 1918—Weather: Cooler

To S.S. as usual. Viv came over to dinner, then we went to see Douglas Fairbanks at the Paramount and home through the park. Gee Wilikuns![72], but I'm tired.

Douglas Fairbanks at the Paramount, *Salt Lake Tribune*, 16 June 1918, page 54.

Monday, 17 June 1918—Weather: Just right.

Spent noon with Laura. Went to school again. It was good to get back. Heard a short concert by the 20th Infantry band. Received a nice letter from Joseph Evans. He is surely in love with Laura.

Tuesday, 18 June 1918—Weather:

Attended the organ recital at the tabernacle. It was very good. The home folks & myself visited Le and Ruby. Spent a very delightful evening.

Wednesday, 19 June 1918—Weather:

Oh joy! But this surely is a slow day. No one in the office but me. Wish someone would come and see me. I can't go out to see them. Went to school and started on my second test. It sure is hot work. The test is easy but long.

Thursday, 20 June 1918—Weather: Hot as the dickens.

I am in the office alone again. Nothing to do until tonight. Then I sew. Received a letter from Shirley Stewart and one from Edward E. Curtis. Both in the Coast Artilary at Cal. I wrote to Clearence Peterson.

Friday, 21 June 1918—Weather:

Went to Dr. Thomas and had my teeth done. Wrote both the boys. Finished my shorthand test. Made 95%. Worse than the first. But it was a harder test.

> Along the margin of the page for 20 and 21 June, Anna wrote: "Shirley, I love you. I love your letters. I love your lovely brown eyes."

Saturday, 22 June 1918—Weather: Slightly stormy.

Saw Viv. Home & sewed on Mrs. B.'s dress. She & Mrs. Spooner came. A letter came from Edgar B. Trass. I don't think I like him much. He is one I met at the depot. Shirley is the only one worth while to me.

> At this point I have not been able to better identify Ann's new beau. All of the Shirleys in the draft registration records were either married, too old, or had registered after the month of June.

Sunday, 23 June 1918—Weather:

Had lunch with Viv and Isabell at Steward's. Then walked in park with Viv and enjoyed concert. I met a nice fellow named Jack. He had lovely eyes.

Monday, 24 June 1918—Weather:

Spent noon with Viv. Laura & I stayed up till one A.M. sewing on Mrs. Byerline's dress.

Tuesday, 25 June 1918—Weather:

Spent noon with Laura. Met Viv. Bought a new green & white bathing suit. Caught the 6:30 train for Saltair & had a nice bath in [the Great Salt] Lake. Returned home by 12 [A]M. A letter from Joe Evans.

Wednesday, 26. June 1918—Weather:

Saw Viv at noon. Went with family on a picknic. Heard band concert at the park.

Thursday, 27 June 1918—Weather:

Met Viv, Laura & Violet and went to the Strand Theatre. *I Hear Val Jean* was the play[73]. Then spent P.M. with Viv at Stewarts. Mr. Brethower called on Laura. Some one phoned for me. I don't know who he was. Sad but true. I'm sure he must be sad to leave town without my last farewell.

Les Miserables played at the Strand for one day only, *Salt Lake Tribune*, 27 June 1918, page 9.

Friday, 28 June 1918—Weather: Hot and then some.

Went to depot and bid goodbye to the 20th Infantry[74]. I suppose we will never see them again. There are only about 450 men at Ft. Douglas now. The town surely seems deserted. I hope they send some more here soon.

Saturday, 29 June 1918—Weather:

The first U.S. troops have arrived in Italy[75]. They were received with a flowery and hilarious reception. Saw Wallace Reed in the Fire Fly of France.[76] It was fine. Oswin Rands in France sent me a copy of the Stars & Stripes[77] from "over there."

The Official Newspaper of the A. E. F.

The Stars and Stripes

By and For the Soldiers of the A. E. F.

15,000 TROOPS, ON BOARD 18 TRANSPORTS, SAILED FROM NEW YORK YEAR AGO TODAY AS FIRST FIGHTING CONTINGENT OF A.E.F.

THE WAVES OF THE ATLANTIC

The front page of the semi-monthly *Stars and Stripes* newspaper for 14 June 1918, published in Paris, possibly the edition Oswin Rands sent to Anna.

Sunday, 30 June 1918—Weather:

To S.S. as usual. Le & Ruby called. Viv came over and we went walking. Laura & I went up to S's [probably Stewart's restaurant] after and had a burglur scare. I had a revolver on that account.[78]

7

JULY
Sewed and Wished I Was 'Over There'

Monday, 1 July 1918—Weather:

Nothing much doing over here. I'd like to be "over there" for a little while. Home early. Received a very interesting letter from Shirley. He surely is a dear old kid.

Tuesday, 2 July 1918—Weather: Hot & sultry.

Viv came to dinner with us and then we each wrote a letter out on the lawn to the soldier boys and also made war on the mosquitoes. One beautiful night.

Wednesday, 3 July 1918—Weather: Sultry again.

Spent noon with Viv. Sewed again.

Thursday, 4 July 1918 - Weather: Nice & warm.

Sewed until six o'clock. Clearence Peterson has come clear from Idaho to see me. He called & took Viv & I to Saltair. Had a nice time. I was a little dissapointed in him.

It is surprising that Anna makes no reference to any kind of Fourth of July celebration. Being a Thursday, it was a legal holiday with most businesses closed and a day off work for Anna, since she sewed all day and went to the Saltair resort—where the biggest crowds were expected. On the next day she mentions going back to work. A search of the *Salt Lake Tribune* for this day did not turn up a single reference to any sort of celebration anywhere in the city, although fireworks were scheduled at the baseball field. The nearest celebrations mentioned were 40 miles to the north in Odgen. On page two of the Salt Lake *Deseret News* was an article about a reporter who went looking about the city for signs of a celebration and reported a small child on the grounds of the Red Cross Headquarters who was marching around waving two of her own flags.

Wee Salt Laker Has Celebration In Her Own Way

Salt Lake had a big Fourth of July celebration this morning. Practically none of the town's citizens knew about it, but as a tribute to the spirit of '76 it probably could not have been bettered. A reporter out after a Fourth of July story had found little by way of patriotic celebration brewing. All the patriotic citizens of the city seemed to be resting on their oars for the day after the week's business cares and ever increasing war burdens, a large majority of them hurrying in automobiles canyonwards or preparing for a day's outing at nearby resorts. The national colors on

An unusual subdued 4th of July celebration in Salt Lake City, exemplified by a small child marching alone, *Deseret News*, 4 July 1918, page 2.

In contrast, an article on page one of the same newspaper made note of countrywide Fourth of July celebrations throughout Britain commemorating the million American soldiers sent to fight against the Germans.

Friday, 5 July 1918—Weather: rain in A.M. also P.M.

Back to work again. Started a sweater for the Red Cross. Met a couple of fellows from the "Cullen"[79] and they came over & chated, for the doctor is out of town. Had lunch with Peterson. Went to Lagoon with Pete, Laura & Walter & Hertha Cerstons. Had a dandy time. Water fine.

The Lagoon is an amusement park located about 25 miles north of Anna's home. It was billed as the "Coney Island of the West." Originally located on the shores of the Great Salt Lake, it was moved to encompass some freshwater ponds closer to Salt Lake City and to avoid being left surrounded by mud when the waters of the Great Salt Lake receded.

A *Utah History Encyclopedia* article by John S. McCormick stated, "At its opening Lagoon advertised 'Bowling, Elegant Dancing Pavilion, Fine Music, A Shady Bowery and Good Restaurants.' Since then other attractions, typical of those found at amusement parks throughout the country, have been added. At one time or another, Lagoon has offered hot-air balloon rides, boxing and wrestling matches, great names in entertainment, horse racing and pari-mutuel betting, roller-skating, baseball games, dancing, swimming, bicycle racing, a zoo, motion pictures, live theater, minstrel shows, rodeos, a midway, row boating, marching bands, wild West shows, fireworks, and mechanical rides."

By 1918, Lagoon was immensely popular for summertime activities, and still exists at this writing. In 1921, a large wooden roller coaster was added that was a source of great fun when I was a boy visiting family in Utah in the summertime in the 1940s and 1950s.

Saturday, 6 July 1918—Weather:

Pete came in and spent an hour & a half in the office with me. Had a jolly time. Met Viv then bade him ta ta and went home and sewed. Too bad to see a perfectly elegable fellow go when the town's so dead.

Sunday, 7 July 1918—Weather:

Stayed home all day. Took a good nap on the lawn.

Monday, 8 July 1918—Weather:

Spent fornoon writing letters in office. Lunched with Viv & Bert. Visited Winn. Mother & I attended the Utah boy's band concert at the Tab. Our soldier boys are stationed at Camp Kearny, Cal[80]. The concert was absohosolutly splendid. Magnificent immense!

Tuesday, 9 July 1918—Weather: [see below]

Went to movie with Viv. Just reach[ed] home in time to avoid the rain. It was sure some rain too. No mail today. The Merchants Bank went closed today[81]. I'm glad my millions are elsewhere.

Wednesday, 10 July 1918—Weather: Slightly threatening rain.

Walk home with Viv. and visited Schultez's & Viv's cousins on the way. A letter from Edgar Grass and one from Joey [her cousin, Joseph Evans] from Idahoy.

Thursday, 11 July 1918—Weather: Cooler today.

Home and sewed. Viv came over and we started her dress. A letter from Pete, a very nice friendly sort.

Friday, 12 July 1918—Weather:

Nothing much doing today. I wonder what the boys "over there" are doing[82]. Viv came over and tried to sew on her dress.

Saturday, 13 July 1918—Weather:

Same here only worse. Went to school for a change.

Sunday, July 14, 1918—Weather: Lovely day. A little shower.

Visited Mrs. Margetts with Viv, Laura and Vivian Kuhn. Had our futures fortold. Nothing dashing but a married man, late at night and a auto ride. Sound bad for a minister's daughter.

Kamp Kearney, California, mobilization site of many members of the 40th Division.

Monday, 15 July 1918—Weather:

Viv & I walked out at noon. The Germans have started another big attack. They have gained on the French some, but the Yankees are pushing them back. 50 miles of [fighting]. Went to school.

Tuesday, 16 July 1918—Weather: Pleasant day.

Saw Laura & Viv at noon. The Yanks are still gaining on the Huns. Viv came over in P.M.

Wednesday, 17 July 1918—Weather:

The Yankees are doing fine work. They'll show them damned Germans. Laura & I walked up to see Viv. Looks like Bert's in love.

Oswin Rands, with the 107th Ammunition Train, along with six other field artillery units was sent into the part of the battle area under the control of the French Seventh Army, which was the front between the Swiss border and Lorraine. The specific purpose was to function as the divisional artillery of the 32nd Division.

Thursday, 18 July 1918—Weather:

Not much doing over here[83]. But lots doing "over there." The Yanks have yanked twelve miles or I mean towns from the Boches[84]. Have gained six miles all along. Everyone "rejoicing." We all slept out on the lawn under the Stars. I received my Liberty Bond.

Friday, 19 July 1918—Weather: Sort of sultry.

The U.S.S. *San Diego* was sunk[85]. Paraded with other R.C. [Red Cross] canteen members with 350 Italians[86] who have been rescued from an Austrian prison camp in Siberia. Now they are going valiantly back to fight. I didn't have my uniform, but you bet I went anyhow. Nothing like it.

The front lines of the 32d Division were raided by a German unit on July 19, while the division was in the Center Sector [Centre]. The raiding party in this operation was repulsed, leaving two prisoners in American hands.

Saturday, 20 July 1918—Weather:

Sissons has been captured by the Allies[87]. Hooray!!! Home at 2:30 P.M. Sewed on Adelaide's dress. Viv came over. Mack called then I met him. He surely is crazy. Just got out of the "Mill" Guard House[88]. I hope he transfers and goes to France. Card from Jesse Evans. He is going "over there."

Sunday, 21 July 1918—Weather:

Had photo taken with S. School. Nearly melted. Walked up to Schultzes with Viv & Bert while Laura went motoring with Sherman. She surely did look charming. Eve's husband is here on a furlough.

Monday, 22. July 1918—Weather:

The Allies are still beating back the Huns. A soft letter from Edward B. Curtis.

Tuesday, 23 July 1918—Weather:

Same here. Attended the concert at Ft. Douglas by the Utah Boy's Band[89]. There were nine in our party. We saw Mack. We had a very nice time. The soldiers served iced tea & cake. But we didn't see the cake.

Wednesday, 24 July 1918—Weather:

Pioneer Day.

Attended Utah Boy's concert in Park. B.H. Roberts[90] spoke. Met many people we knew. Laura, June & I attended the same boy's concert at the Capital Building in evening. Also the dance. The only thing lacking was soldiers. I shook hands with the Governor[91] & the band master[92], but I am in love with the fat singer.

Pioneer Day is the state holiday in Utah commemorating the arrival of the first Mormon pioneers in the Salt Lake Valley, 24 July 1847. Normally the 24th of July festivities throughout the state were all about the dwindling number of remaining "Forty-Seveners." But in 1918, the activities were also filled with tributes to the men in the military. Indeed, when the governor spoke at the gathering at Liberty Park where Anna spent the day, he exclaimed, "Everything is war just now." In addition, he compared the sacrifices of the pioneers in 1847 to the sacrifices being made by the thousands of men from

Utah then sacrificing their lives for democracy in France. He told of the "French women who are teaching their children to care for the graves of Americans, as they do for the graves of the French who fall in battle." Anna didn't mention in her diary that one of her nearby neighbors, 80 year-old Sarah J. Rich Miller, was one of the remaining original pioneers. *Deseret News*, 24 Jul 1918, page 9.

Thursday, 25 July 1918—Weather:

Back to work again as per usual. The Allies have a half-million Germans in a pocket[93]. The b[l]oodiest battle of all is yet to come.

Friday, 26 July 1918—Weather:

Attended a very informal wedding reception on Joe Smith and his wife. He goes to a training camp tommorrow. Bessie Evans is visiting us from Idaho. I like [her] very much. First time we ever met. A card came from Bob Mead. Also a letter from Sergt. Chapla.

Saturday, 27 July 1918—Weather:

Hurried home at 2 and got busy and cleaned house. A nice letter was waiting for me from Shirley Stewart. He is now at Camp Devins, Virginia[94].

As of this date, the 107th Ammunition Train was located at Aisne-Marne, until 6 August, which made it directly involved in the Second Battle of the Marne. The Second Battle of the Marne lasted from 15 July to 6 August 1918. Conceived as an attempt to draw Allied troops south from Flanders to facilitate an attack in that region, the offensive along the Marne proved to be the last the German Army would mount in the war. In the opening days of the fighting, German forces made only minor gains before being halted by a constellation of Allied troops.

"Due to intelligence gathering, the Allies were largely aware of

German intentions and had prepared a sizable counter-offensive. This moved forward on July 18 and quickly shattered German resistance. After two days of fighting, the Germans commenced a retreat back to trenches between the Aisne and Vesle [r]ivers. The Allied attack was the first in a series of sustained offensives that would bring the war to an end that November." (Kennedy Hickman, ThoughtCo.com.)

Sunday, 28 July 1918—Weather:

Stayed home all day for a change. Had a self home-made concert in the hammock. The members of the band were Laura, Violet & I. The audience was Don, Walter and Donna. Oh! I am so tired.

The battle at Belleau Wood was fought primarily by the U.S. Marine Corps; the U.S. Army was there too, and the Marines suffered more casualties in that battle than it did in its entire history to that point. Belleau Wood was about 30 miles northeast of Paris, and with the Allied victory after weeks of intense carnage, the German Army was repulsed, and Paris was saved. Their success at Belleau Wood merited an immortal place in Marine Corps history and lore.

The Aisne-Marne American Cemetery, near the Belleau Wood battleground, in Belleau, Northern France. 1,800 U.S. Marines are buried here.

Monday, 29 July 1918—Weather: (See below)

Hurried home and sewed on Mrs. Byerline's cloths [95]. She came over for a fitting. Mrs. Odbert also came. Laura & I visited Viv & Bert at 9:30 P.M. Had a jolly two hours. Getting hotter weather now.

Tues. July 30, 1918—Weather: Gee! I'm nearly suffocated.

The Germans have beaten the Americans out of two towns[96]. "Oh God! be with us yet, Lest we forget."

Anna appears to be recalling from memory the refrain from "Recessional," a poem by Rudyard Kipling, which he composed on the occasion of Queen Victoria's Diamond Jubilee in 1897, and which appeared in the 1909 Mormon hymnal *Deseret Sunday School Songs*, no. 283, "God of Our Fathers": "Lord God of Hosts, be with us yet, Lest we forget—lest we forget!" The first of the five stanzas:

> *God of our fathers, known of old,*
> *Lord of our far-flung battle line,*
> *Beneath whose awful hand we hold*
> *Dominion over palm and pine,*
> *Lord God of Hosts, be with us yet,*
> *Lest we forget, lest we forget!*

Wednesday, 31 July 1918—Weather: Still hot.

Our boys are gaining again. I am wondering whether I should be a nurse or not. My country is calling and my home and mother is calling. Will I be of more value to stay and finish my business education or shall I enlist in W. S. [War Service] training school.

YOUNG WOMEN URGED TO JOIN NURSES' CORPS

Enrollment for Student Reserve Corps Begins Actively This Morning

The student nurse reserve campaign officially begins today. All young women in the city who wish actively to help out the government in one of its most crying needs at the present time are urged to identify themselves with the student nurse reserve corps.

Call for more nurses for War Service extends to students to register for training, *Salt Lake Herald*, 29 July 1918, page 12.

8

AUGUST
TOO YOUNG TO GO, AND SHIRLEY IS OUT

Thursday, 1 August 1918—Weather: [See below]

Wrote a card to Aunt Emma[97] in Logan. Secured literature about nursing. Very undecided. Laura and I walked up to Byerline's then to Taggart's. Pleasant, [cool] evening.

Friday, 2 August 1918—Weather:

Tryed to find Ruby at noon but failed. Instead I found a woman with a toothache. I bought the lunch for tomorrow. I surely had some dashing time before the stores closed. I had a time getting my check cashed. I nearly was arrested for fast walking.

Saturday, 3 August 1918—Weather:

Laura and I attended the Ft. Douglas field day. Saw all kinds of contests and sports including Mack. Spent afternoon with a jolly Idaho boy named Thomas Spurgeon. Ate our basket lunch with Mr. Vinton and Rufus Tolman, a cow puncher from Ida. Had a wonderful time.

Sunday, 4 August 1918—Weather:

Daddy and I escorted Mother and Don to depot where we bid so long, as they are going to take a vacation in [Cache] Valley [in Northern Utah, near

Logan]. Came home and envited Tom to dinner to taste my first cooking. He surely is a nice jolly boy. We have adopted him as our big sister Tom.

Monday, 5 August 1918—Weather:

I am remaining at home this week to keep house. I really enjoy it but it certainly keeps one dashing every minute to keep house. Viv came over. She has decided to become a nurse. Wish I could.

Tuesday, 6 August 1918—Weather:

Nothing exciting as yet except that the folks still exist through the cooking. Vivian and Bert called. Eunice Woodruff[98] came from [Cache] Valley to see us. She is offering her services to Uncle Sam at Washington D.C.

Wednesday, 7 August 1918—Weather:

Went to the Park with folks to picnic with Seventies quorum[99]. Met Shorty Tolman. He lunched with us then we all went rowing. Had a dandy time. He gave Lal and I each a photo of himself. It is certainly nice.

From this date, the 107th Ammunition Train was relocated to Fismes, Champagne, between Paris and the border with Belgium, until 17 August. It was here where the last vestiges of the Second Battle of the Marne were fought between the 32nd Division and the retreating German troops.

Thursday, 8 August 1918—Weather:

Violet, Eunice & I went to the Orpheum to see "The Hearts of the World." It is a wonderful war picture. Best I have yet seen. Bessie Evans came in the evening. After supper we all fussed around in the hammock and laughed and sang.

D. W. Griffith's *Hearts of the World* at the Orpheum Theater, *Salt Lake Tribune*, 6 August 1918, page 9.

Friday, 9 August 1918—Weather:

Eunice left on the eight o'clock train. I spent afternoon sewing on Mrs. Odberts skirts. Bud or Bessie is a jolly little girl. I received another letter from France[100], near the firing line. He said there was an air deul going on right over him.

Saturday, 10 August 1918—Weather:

Worked like Trojians cleaning house until five P.M. We said good bye to

Bud and met Mack. He went shopping with us then he and I spent evening at Lagoon. We had a nice time. Now I know I'm crazy. The train was late, so we had to come home in a taxi.

Sunday, 11 August 1918—Weather:

I gave the [Sunday school] lesson in my class. They have given us a few more pupils. It was a good lesson and I enjoyed it. I believe the kiddoes like me better each time. Mack phoned. Laura & I strolled in the Park. Viv & Bert are making their nursing uniforms. Wish I was too.

The 107th Ammunition Train was relocated to Courmont, France, southward near the border with Switzerland on 11 August 1918.

Monday, 12 August 1918—Weather:

Hit the hay early for a change.

Tuesday, 13 August 1918—Weather:

Same here. Now I want to go to France as a cheer girl, to cheer the Sammy's as they come out of the hospitals.

Wednesday, 14 August 1918—Weather: [see below]

Guess I can't after all. Oh, such a blow. I am too young by five years. Ah me. Lauretta & little Allen & Glenna came from Denver. I was surely ticklled to see them. Glenna is Hal over again. We had a late dinner. I could squeeze the babies to death, almost. A little rain. 700 soldier engineers arrived[101]. Goody.

The 107th Ammunition train was moved again—to Gossoncourt Woods, France[102], on 14 August.

Wanted--Girls Cheerful, Good Pals, Not Fat

ARE you a cheer maker? Then again are you fat, spelled s t o u t ? "Nobody loves a fat man" has been the cry and the sermon, and the song and the theme of philosophers and song writers, cynics and preachers, since the beginning of the world, at least since people started dieting on 100 per cent caloried foods.

But just to show how deeply ingrained in popular wisdom the little doctrine is, comes the latest admonition from the Red Cross headquarters. This is the way the headlines read, "Wanted — 500 cheer-makers, who must be strong, self-reliant, cheerful and not stout."

The Red Cross organization decided to put out a call for cheerful women who would work at the hospitals in France to cheer up wounded soldiers. They needed to be at least 25 years old and could not be overweight. *Salt Lake Herald*, 13 August 1918, page 5.

Thursday, 15 August 1918—Weather:

Nothing dashing doing. Only little Allen and Glenna are the life of the household. I have to do some tall hustling to keep house as well as get to work on time. The first Yankee troops have landed in Russia[103].

Friday, 16 August 1918—Weather:

We all picniced at the Park. The babies kept us always interested. The "Areal" quartet entertained. They are surely fine. Had a nice time and went home tired. The boys are still gaining ground. There are a few young women wearing overalls about town.

Saturday, 17 August 1918 - Weather: We are having pleasant cool weather now.

Lauretta, Laura & I went to Saltair. Met Ruby out there and had a nice time. I was lucky at the horses and won a box of candy. Phoned mother at Smithfield to stay longer.

Sunday, 18 August 1918—Weather:

Lauretta went to Ogden at six. Ruby & I accompanied her to the train. We hit the hay early. Lauretta is surely a peach of a girl. I surely wish she lived here.

> The 107th Ammunition Train was being relocated back up to Oise-Aisne, between Paris and the Belgian border, until 6 September, where the final stages of the Aisne-Marne campaign were fought, and a threat to Paris was ended.

Monday, 19 August 1918—Weather:

Letter from Shirley Stewart. I don't like him anymore. He talks about himself too much. Home and to bed early. Japan is having rice riots[104] in all large towns. The new conscription laws[105] will make the W.S. 4 million strong in June and we will win the war by 1920[106]. I frantically hope so.

Tuesday, 20 August 1918—Weather:

To work as per usual. Nothing much doing here, but everything doing "over there." They have the Fritzies[107] on the run to Hunland (Germany).

Wednesday, 21 August 1918—Weather: Cooler today.

I am home the rest of this week to clean house before mother arrives. Violet & I washed today and also cleaned the front bedroom.

Thursday, 22 August 1918—Weather:

I am surely getting my fill of house work. We done the parlor today. Too tired at night to venture out.

Friday, 23 August 1918—Weather:

Same here only shifted to the back bedroom and kitchen.

Saturday, 24 August 1918—Weather:

A finish of everything. Mack phoned. Mother came home at eight P.M. She is indeed absoposolutly welcome. She looks much better and Don[108] is minus a front tooth.

Sunday, 25 August 1918—Weather

Mack came with two handsome horses at 2 P.M. We road all afternoon and had a delightful time. "Shorty" Rufus Tolman called on Laura and they road while we finished then we [took] the horses back to the fort and strolled home.

Monday, 26 August 1918—Weather:

Mother has Le's boy Max to care for while Le and Ruby are away on a trip. I wish something exciting would happen. We received two letters from Bill. One a month old and the other two mon. old. He is still in South America and enjoying himself.

Tuesday, 27 August 1918—Weather:

Nothing dashing but the baby squacked its share.

Wednesday, 28 August 1918—Weather:

Borrowed ($50.00) fifty dollars and placed it to my acct. for my schooling. Bill is my victim. Laura, Rufus Tolman & I attended the Military wedding at Saltair. Had a dandy supper dance after at the Ship Cafe. Met nice people and had a rippin' time.

A Most Unique Wedding
—AT—
SALTAIR
On Auerbach Day
Wednesday, August 28th, at 8:45 p.m. in the Roller Skating Rink.

Promising to be one of the most brilliant events of this mammoth celebration is the wedding in public of Private Nat H. Elliott of B company, 23d battalion, U. S. guards, and Miss Charlotte Malone of Oakland, Cal., scheduled to take place in the evening, so that all those working in the day may have an opportunity to view this interesting event. There will be a military escort of seventy-five soldiers, with thirty pretty girls in the bridal procession. Be sure and witness this unusual wedding.

EVERYBODY INVITED

Announcement for a public "Military Wedding" at Saltair — a publicity event for the Auerbach department store, *Salt Lake Herald-Republican*, 25 August 1918, page 7.

Thursday, 29 August 1918—Weather:

Nothing exciting today.

Friday, 30 August 1918—Weather:

Nor today.

Saturday, 31 August 1918—Weather:

Spent afternoon with Viv. She enters hospitel training tonight. I almost wish I were too. Received a card from Jack Quinn. He is soon to go "over there."

9

SEPTEMBER
A Souvenir from No Man's Land

Sunday, 1 September 1918—Weather:

Laura and I walked to the Park in evening and studied spelling. We met Earl Cushman and Jesse Marryhue. Had a jolly time with them. I was back to my days of seventeen. It's lots of fun.

Monday, 2 September 1918—Weather: Rained all afternoon.

This Labor Day. We surely labored. We at home and dad in the parade. Maud & June Smith & others visited us and then Shorty and his friend took Lal & I to the Lake. We slipped Whitiker and had a good time. Home early.

Tuesday, 3 September 1918—Weather:

I am in the office alone as the doctor has gone on a honey moon[109]. "I hope he has a wonderful time."

Wednesday, 4 September 1918—Weather:

Mack and I attended the Tabernacle organ recital then he spent the afternoon. He's a funny guy.

Thursday, 5 September 1918—Weather:

He came unexpectedly again during the afternoon. Brought me some chocolates.

Friday, 6 September 1918 - Weather:

Still alone. Went joy riding with Kershaw and the girls. Saw Viv's residence. Surely is nice. Laura & I walked out after. Mack called.

Saturday, 7 September 1918—Weather:

Mack called. Home at three P.M. after a little shopping tour. I sewed on my blue dress.

Sunday, 8 September 1918—Weather: Rain in fornoon.

Mr. Stolls called while I was gone. To Sunday School as usual. Had dinner at one thirty. I went horse back riding with Mack at two. We journeyed out to Millcreek Canyon. It is certainly a wonderful, beautiful place. We had a delightful time and ate a lot of peaches. Arrived home at 8 P.M.

Monday, 9 September 1918—Weather:

Mack called in A.M. I fear I shall go to school tonight. I arose at 4:30 A.M. and started washing. I am rather pokey today.

Tuesday, 10 September 1918—Weather:

Mack spent afternoon in the office with me. We painted him a mustache. It certainly is becoming. Le & Angus Woodruff called on us. Mack and Angus took Laura and I to the Odeon. Had a glamdorius time.

> The 107th Ammunition train was moved to La Folie, France, in the Joinville area.

Wednesday, 11 September 1918—Weather:

Nothing much doing today. I went to a movie at noon. Elsie Furgeson is surely beautiful[110]. Went to school. Rufus Tolman was visiting Laura when I arrived home. He is to leave town very soon. Poor kid I like him.

Thursday, 12 September 1918—Weather:

This is the day all men between the ages of 18 and 21 and 31 to 45 are to register for W.S. service. So it is a legal holiday. I am home all day but busier than ever.

Friday, 13 September 1918—Weather:

Mack called on the phone. I don't like him one bit. I went to school and he met me after. We walked home. A very peculiar walk indeed. We visited Mr. Parker & his wife. Then the grand parting. He still says I am the only girl. I heard him whistling "Don't you ever feel lonely."

Saturday, 14 September 1918—Weather:

I surely like Mack though. Even if we can't agree. He came in to pay a little debt to me and he looked so blue I had to laugh at him. We went out and walked till three o'clock. He wanted to sluff a date for me but I went right away and left him. No man's going to sluff any girl for me. We had a grand time even if we were supposed to be mad.

Sunday, 15 September 1918—Weather:

We entertained three University training soldier boys at dinner and home. We all had a great time. Mr. Frank Carson, Corp. Wm. Jones, and Mr. Fred Braithwaite. All dandy Utah boys preparing to serve their Uncle Sammy.

Monday, 16 September 1918—Weather:

Well I guess I'm deserted now. I go lonely, wearily to school and no one to care whither or whence. Oh! I received a letter from Clearance Peterson, but he don't count any more. The only time he writes is when there is no one else or nothing else.

Tuesday, 17 September 1918—Weather:

I'm in the office still alone. I wish something interesting or at least dashing would happen. The only thing new is I have on a different combination of dress today. Red hat & tie. Navy blue dress & black fur scarf. It is quite becoming. I heard the organ today.

Wednesday, 18 September 1918—Weather: [See below]

I should go to school but I feel so odd that I can't study. No use going unless I have my lessons prepared. I walked through the Park on my way home. A beautiful perfect day. Jesse Maryhue & Earl Cushman came and invited Laura & I to a party Sat. We were surely surprised.

Thursday, 19 September 1918—Weather:

Nothing doing today but I am doing my shorthand. Johny Smith called on us this evening. I was good to see him again. He is the same old Johnny boy as ever with his jovial carefree out door ways. He was never meant to work in an office.

Friday, 20 September 1918—Weather:

Back to school again. Vivian was at the house when I returned. She likes nursing fine and I believe she is getting heavier than ever.

Saturday, 21 September 1918—Weather:

Spent quite some time phoning and making engagements for the Doc as he is coming from his honeymoon Mon. Laura & I went to a party with Earl Cushman and his crowd at a private place on the West side. Had a nice time but they are too young and *soft*.

Sunday, 22 September 1918—Weather: Rain all day long.

Nothing special doing only Laura sang in church. Mr. & Mrs. Berg called and made us late for church.

> The 107th Ammunition Train was located at Avocourt (Lorraine), France, until 25 September.

Monday, 23 September—Weather:

To school again.

Tuesday, 24 September 1918—Weather:

Stayed home all evening.

Wednesday, 25 September 1918—Weather:

To school again.

Thursday, 26 September 1918—Weather:

Can't remember what.

> From this point until Armistice Day, 11 November 1918, the 107th Ammunition Train was serving in Meuse-Argonne, a region eastward toward the border with Germany.

Friday, 27 September 1918—Weather:

To school and home early and to dance in ward with Dad & Laura and Violet. Fair time.

Saturday, 28 September 1918—Weather:

Laura & I met Vivian too late to see the Liberty Loan Auto parade[111] so we went to the Odeon[112]. Genevie also went. We had a nice time. Today starts the big Fourth Loan drive. The day was ushered in with rifle shots, whistles, & boy scouts with "extras."

Sunday, 29 September 1918—Weather:

We entertained two Eastern boys from Fort Douglas at dinner. We had a jolly time. The objective is $9,000,000,000. Utah alone must furnish $18,000,000. Some bunch, believe me.

Monday, 30 September 1918—Weather:

Mother, Violet & I took part in the great Liberty Pagent. Had a jolly time and came home tired. Bulgaria has surrendered unconditionally. This is the beginning of the defeat of the Central Powers. Received a souvenier from "No Man's Land" from O.P.R[113].

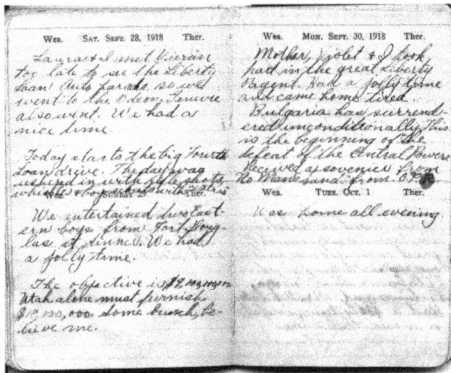

A sample page from Anna's diary, 28 September–1 October 1918.

10

OCTOBER
ALL PUBLIC MEETINGS POSTPONED

Tuesday, 1 October 1918—Weather:

Was home all evening.

Wednesday, 2 October 1918—Weather:

Back to school again. Received a smart letter from Laurence Weber in Cali. and it made me very angry. Shall I answer it.

Thursday, 3 October 1918—Weather:

Nothing dashing. The most interesting Southerner who can tell great... stories called on us with his friend. 'Alabama Slim' Coleman Perkins and Mr. Whitaker. Had a jolly time, in fact, a wonderful time.

Friday, 4 October 1918—Weather:

To school then to the Y.W.C.A. to take military training under Col. Wright[114]. It certainly is fun. Home at ten P.M.

Saturday, 5 October 1918—Weather:

Lauretta came also Margarete Edwards. We all with Vivian K. went to the Odeon[115]. Had a wonderful time. We met lots of rubes[116]. Hit the hay about 1 [A.M.].

Sunday, 6 October 1918—Weather: Rain all fornoon.

Alabama Slim came at three o'clock. He is surely an entertaining fellow. We all laughed so hard we [ached] all over. Uncle Ed Edward came. Germany is asking for Peace[117]. The soft thing. We will show them a little.

Monday, 7 October 1918—Weather:

Met Viv. She has quite the hospital. I knew she liked a good time too well. Also met Eve. To school then to Y.W.C.A. for more militaire. I certainly like it but I am too busy with school to continue it.

Tuesday, 8 October 1918[118] —Weather:

Lauretta spent all afternoon with me in the office. I wrote a stiff letter to L.J. Weber. Home early and sewed on Evelyn's dress. To bed at 1:30 A.M. At any rate I finished it. Slim called for a few minutes to bring some pictures.

Wednesday, 9 October 1918[119]—Weather:

Met my old school friend Maxine Maxon. Glad to see her. Also met Mack. He wants me to go horseback riding with him again. He also said I am still the only girl. Ha Ha. We were badly dissapointed on a dance on account of the Spanish Influenza epidemic[120]. No dance, no nothing. Alabama Slim came any how.

Thursday, 10 October 1918—Weather:

All public meeting of any kind are postponed on account of the Flue epidemic[121]. Churches, theatres, dances and every thing both public and private. When I arrived home at five o'clock, Tom Spurgeon was visiting Laura. We had a jolly time but he's too soft and fresh too.

UTAH BANS ALL MEETINGS

TRIES TO CURB INFLUENZA

BARS AMUSEMENT DOORS

TO combat the spread of Spanish influenza throughout Utah, Dr. T. B. Beatty, state health officer, issued yesterday an order, effective today, closing theatres, schools, churches and other institutions and assemblies which bring together concourses of persons.

The order was issued with the concurrence of the state board of health, which approved Dr. Beatty's action at a special session, held at noon in the Alta club.

Dr. Ernest A. Smith, superintendent of the Salt Lake schools, announced that the order will be observed in this city and the schools of Salt Lake will not open this morning. The Ogden board of education, according to Supt. Henry C. Johnson of the Ogden schools, will disregard the order. While refusing to believe that the state board had taken action, Mr. Johnson declared last night that the Ogden schools will remain open "in any event."

Salt Lake Has 63 Cases

According to Dr. Samuel C. Paul, city physician, there were in Salt Lake last night a total of sixty-three reported cases of the disease. No deaths were reported in the state yesterday.

No time limit was placed by Dr. Beatty on the closing order. He expressed the hope, however, that the restrictions may be lifted within a week or ten days.

The closing order will affect all schools, including the University of Utah and the Utah Agricultural college. At the University of Utah thirty cases were extant yesterday, according to Lieutenant Grace, medical officer of the students' army training corps unit of the university. The patients were sent to the Fort Douglas hospital.

1000 Students to Mark Time

About 1000 students at the school will be held back by the order. Men registered in the vocational section and those who live on the campus will remain at their quarters. Dr. John A. Widtsoe, president of the university,

(Continued on Page 7.)

Steps taken in health order to prevent spread of the epidemic, *Salt Lake Herald-Republican*, 10 October 1918, page 1.

One column to the left on the same front page of the *Herald-Republican* ran an editorial exclaiming that the pandemic was a hoax, and accusing the newspapers of yellow journalism and the physicians of fear mongering.

Friday, 11 October 1918—Weather:

[H.S.] & Pvt. Kramer of the 70th Engineers, Ft. Douglas came for the evening. Had a real nice time. But I like Kramer better. Lauretta has gone back to Ogden now. Germany is seriously considering Pres. Wilson's peace plans. I hope no peace comes yet until the Germans realize the wrongs they have done.

EPIDEMIC IS NOT SERIOUS

PRECAUTION, NOT PANIC

NO REASON FOR ALARM

(AN EDITORIAL)

BETWEEN local yellow journalism and an over excited public we are in danger of being scared into a sickness that ordinary precaution and common sense should avoid. There is not the slightest occasion for panic in Salt Lake City over the alleged epidemic of Spanish influenza. A yellow journal made the statement last night that there were SEVERAL HUNDRED CASES IN SALT LAKE CITY, when as a matter of fact the records of the city board of health show sixty-three cases reported up to 9 o'clock last night.

Let the people use ordinary common sense in this matter and refuse to be panic-stricken by dire predictions and false statements. We have been led to believe that the city is threatened with a deadly plague, but the proof is not forthcoming. Now that the fat is in the fire, the state board of health should issue through the newspapers directions for combating the disease, but there should be no more forecasts of mortality which serve only to make well people quite sure they are sick.

When la grippe first made its appearance we went through the same ordeal. Overwrought health departments and overzealous physicians threw a scare into us that put a great many weak-kneed individuals to bed who otherwise would never have thought of being sick. Remain composed and keep confidence. It is unpleasant to be sick and Salt Lake may be in for a share of this sickness, but do not invite it by dire imaginations and worry. The thought should make all people cautious but it should not destroy ordinary horse sense.

It may have been wisdom to close the theatres and churches, although we doubt it. In the interests of safety first it may be all right to close the schools, but under the present system of medical supervision we are inclined to believe that the children are as safe in school as they will be at home or on the streets. At any rate, a little more precaution and less tendency to panic will go a long ways toward guarding the health of the entire community.

Editorial claiming the influenza epidemic was a hoax perpetrated by yellow journalism, *Salt Lake Herald-Republican*, 10 October 1918, page 1.

OGDEN SCHOOL OFFICIALS DEFY CLOSING ORDER

Superintendent Johnson Declares Schools Will Remain Open

Herald Special.

Ogden, Oct. 9.—"We shall open the public schools of Ogden tomorrow, regardless of any order that we have received to date," said Supt. H. C. Johnson of the Ogden schools tonight, when

In defiance of the shut-down order, Ogden schools vowed to remain open. The city of Ogden very soon was forced to block all visitors who did not have health clearances.

Saturday, 12 October 1918—Weather:

Spent lunch with Viv & Bert. Met Evelyne. Utah is short its bond quotta. Today is another bond day. If you haven't a bond you get pushed [off] the walk. Mr. [H.S.] phoned. He's too little to like. Slim took Laura & I to town.

Greatest Patriotic Endeavor to Attain Goal

From early morning until late at night the downtown business section of Salt Lake will swarm with dauntless women and girl campaign workers whose duty it will be to persuade passersby to buy more bonds. The very sidewalks will bear their messages that he who runs may read and in the reading be stirred to greater patriotic endeavor even though he feels already that his purse strings have been drawn their tautest. Bands will play, "stunts" will be staged to draw attention to the need of buying, and every resource of the Liberty loan committees will be strained to the breaking point that the city's vaunted loyalty may remain unsullied by failure in this, the greatest of all loan drives—and the most important.

The women workers are to be given every possible assistance in their efforts at solicitation. Main street and East Broadway will be veritable battle fronts, with trenches erected all along their business blocks. These will be manned by fighting men from Fort Douglas. No Man's Land will lie between the curbs and every passerby who cannot show a Liberty bond button or other evidence of having purchased one or more bonds will be compelled to leave the sidewalk and pass through the danger zone unless he subscribes on the spot.

"They shall not pass" are the orders of the day to be applied to every one who doesn't wear the telltale button or ribbon. Bevies of pretty girls will be at each trench to pounce upon the nonpurchaser. They have orders to stop every passerby and even those wearing the button will not be entirely immune. The password will be the ribbon bearing the words, "I have bought more." This and this only will secure "freedom of the Main and East Broadway seas" to pedestrians.

Liberty Bond sales solicited on two downtown blocks by forcing pedestrians off the sidewalks if they did not have proof of purchasing bonds, *Salt Lake Herald-Republican*, 12 October 1918, page 9.

Sunday, 13 October 1918—Weather:

Vivian Kuhn came. We couldn't even go to church on account of the "flu." Slim came at 2:30. Dined at five and walked to the park in evening. He and I cannot agree very well. I guess he is angry at me now. I should worry. Went to my slumbers at 9:30.

Monday, 14 October 1918—Weather:

Stayed home and sewed all evening. President Wilson has made a great historical step. He has told Germany that their unconditional surrender is the only Peace terms. Everyone is enthusiastic. Utah's Liberty Bond quota is still one & one quarter million short.

Tuesday, 15 October 1918—Weather:

[H.S.] called on me in the evening. He is surely a peculiar fellow. I fear he is going to like me two well. He and Laura & I went walking in the evening. Had a pleasant time.

Wednesday, 16. October 1918—Weather: (See below)

Rushed home and sewed all evening on Vivian K's dress, while mother and Laura spent the evening doing Red Cross work in Sugar House[122]. Heavy rain fall. The influenza is raging everywhere.

Thursday, 17 October 1918—Weather:

Home earley and sewed. Le and Ruby were at the house when I arrived. There was no battle as I expected. Of coarse they are our guests at present. I shall wait and see. There are under surface fires burning, I fear. There are thousands dying from the flu. Ft. Douglas is in quarantine now.

Friday, 18 October 1918—Weather:

Vivian Kuhn called in the evening. I received a letter from Clarence Peterson at Tacoma, Wash. He is still in quarantine. Poor boy.

Saturday, 19 October 1918—Weather:

Met Viv & Bert. [H.S.] phoned. Had a heck of a time over some dad gasted buttons. Rushed madly home and sewed. Received a phony letter from [H.S.].

Sunday, 20 October 1918—Weather:

Sewed all fornoon. Everything is still closed for the flu. Anna Lund, you [are] positively the most impossibly intolerable person I ever met. Better cut it out, you will lose friends fast.

Monday, 21 October 1918—Weather:

Home early and sewed again while Mother and Laura worked at the Red Cross gauze rooms. Le and Ruby have found a house now in Sugar House and are busy preparing it for use. The Germans don't like Pres. Wilson's curt note to their peace plea. Received a box of candy from [H.S.].

Tuesday, 22 October 1918—Weather:

Left the office at 3:30 P.M. for the [D&RG]. depot. At five an immense troop train came in from Camp Fremont, Cal[123]. We served them with apples, bananas, grapes, & cigarettes. Two more trains came. I left dead tired at nine o'clock. But happy.

Wednesday, 23 October 1918—Weather:

This terrible pestilence which is raging all over the earth is taking the lives of thousands. The [cemeteries] are becoming the most popular boulevards and business is booming for the undertakers.

Thursday, 24 October 1918—Weather:

I wish something exciting would happen. There is so much happening "over there." Still we must remain home and avoid the "flu."

Friday, 25 October 1918—Weather:

Laura & I worked in the Red Cross gauze rooms at Sugar House. I enjoyed it immensely. I learned to make two kinds of bandages. One must be very exact and scrutinize closely.

Saturday, 26 October 1918—Weather:

Nothing dashing—only a letter from Douglas Edwards. He is starting across the continent on his way to France. [H.S.] came for the evening. He is indeed a peculiar fellow. I fear he likes me.

Sunday, 27 October 1918—Weather:

Vivian Kuhn came to visit us and get her dress. Then in the evening Laura, Vivian and I went to Shultzs to see Viv P. Had a very pleasant evening.

Monday, 28 October 1918—Weather:

Received another funny letter from "Girley" [H.S.]. Mother and Laura and I went to Red Cross again.

Tuesday, 29 October 1918—Weather:

Home early. Spent evening typewriting. "Girley" called. He is going to leave town soon. I am really glad. Went to depot to bid Bill Jones & Fred Braithwaite ta ta. They are going to Ft. Winfield Scott[124]. They have been in training at the U. of U. [University of Utah].

Wed. 30 October 1918 - Weather:

Alabama Slim and "Girley" [H S] came for the evening. We visited Le and Ruby a little. We surely had a hilarious time singing "You Made Me Love You, I didn't want to do it[125]." [Anna ends this day's entry with a line written in shorthand.]

A line of shorthand for Oct. 30, which translates to, "I still love you, Lawrence, more than ever."

Thursday, 31 October 1918—Weather:

The Turks have surrendered unconditionally. Home early. Practiced on typewriter. Received a letter from Clarence Peterson. I like his stile. Yesterday a letter came from a Sergt. Moreno, a person unknown to me. But I like his stile too so I guess I shall answer. Earl Cushman called and invited Laura and I to a Halloween bon fire party tonight.

11

NOVEMBER
Peace and a Glamdorious Time

Friday, 1 November 1918—Weather.

Laura is 17 today & a beauty. Well we went to the party[126]. We, means Laura, Earl Cushman & Fred Williams & myself. The barn was decorated cutely and we had plenty of "hot dogs" and rolls, doughnuts and marshmellows to bake and good time. Also had my fortune told. I am supposed to get my wish.

No mention of precautionary measures to prevent the spread of the Influenza!

Saturday, 2 November 1918—Weather:

Hurried home and sewed. Received a letter from Oswin Rands in France. Poor kid is lonely for the good old U.S.A. They have the Germans running so fast now that they think it will soon be over. Austria has given up to the Italians opening the back door to Germany for the Allies. Peace will come soon now.

Sunday, 3 November 1918—Weather:

Went to dinner at Stewards. Then visited Shultz's for evening. Slim came to see Laura and Vivian. We took pictures to send to Bill and others for Xmas.

Monday, 4 November 1918—Weather:

The pictures turned out fine. All good but four. The Allies are pushing the Germans back, back, back. But the Huns lay waste to all territory as they evacuate. But Belgium will soon be cleared of their dirty hords. Went to Red Cross with Mother & Laura.

Tuesday, 5 November 1918—Weather:

This is election day. [H.S.] called up and says he is not going away. All the rest of his bunch went but a very few. Tough luck Anna girl. Do better next time.

Wednesday, 6 November 1918—Weather:

Nothing dashing but the Yankee boys over there. The Germans have sent a Peace delegation to Field Marshal Gen. Foch. There is revolution all over Germany, especially among their sailors and marines who have mutinied. "To hell with the Kaiser."

Thursday, 7 November 1918—Weather:

A phony report came out about peace. The country went wild with excitement and joy. Whistles blew, bells rang, parades were held and in some cities the excitement caused deaths. Never have I seen so much enthusiasm spontaniously displayed before.

Friday, 8 November 1918—Weather:

The report was wrong[127]. Such dissapointment. Every thing is more quiet than ever. The German peace delegates met Marshal Foch and don't like his terms. He has given them 72 hrs to answer yes or no. I believe I am more satisfied now than with the sudden peace, for Germany deserves a taste of her own attrocities. [H.S.] came.

Saturday, 9 November 1918—Weather:

Today starts a big War Fund Drive. There has been a parade & street speaking & singing. This is for beneficial necessities & entertainment of our soldier boys & girls who are wining the war too. Lauretta, Hal & Glenna came[128]. First we've seen Hal for two years. They brought us each a gift.

Sunday, 10 November 1918—Weather:

Le & Ruby & Max came to dinner. Also Slim, Mr. Chambers and Mr. Nejadly. We took lots of pictures. Then after dinner went to see Vivan P. Had a delightful time and I like Mr. Chambers fine. They are from the Hospital Corps.

Monday, 11 November 1918—Weather:

Peace!! Peace!! Peace!! The whole country is wild with joy over the wonderful news. Thirty-six hours of the most hillarious celebration I have ever witnessed. I met L.W. on the street. He is much heavier now. Mack called. Had lunch with Hal.

The Salt Lake Tribune's exclamation that Armistice Day drew the greatest crowd in the history of Salt Lake City, *Salt Lake Tribune*, 12 November 1918, page 1.

In the early hours of Monday morning, the American Expeditionary Forces in France were notified of the signing of the Armistice, which signaled a cease-fire across the Western Front of France. The American Expeditionary Forces also had been misled into believing the war had ended on 7 November, and the nighttime blackouts ceased. But the German troops did not take advantage and bombard the exposed Americans.

The American Army was quickly reorganized to create the Third Army, or the III Corps, to become the Army of Occupation. Oswin's division, the 32nd Division, was one of seven U.S. divisions that were included. This confirms family lore that Oswin was part of the Army of Occupation.

Tuesday, 12 November 1918—Weather:

The town has quieted but the wonderful happiness is prevalent for Germany has given up absolutely unconditionally. They are starving to death and asking for food from us. This is the biggest event ever. Germany will be a Republic now.

'FLU' SPREADS OVER CIVILIZED WORLD

Germ Eludes Bacteriologists; Health Authorities Are Baffled.

The influenza epidemic continues unabated. Its ravages are not confined to this city or state, or even to the United States, and cable reports indicate that it is rapidly spreading over the civilized world. It has baffled medical skill to an unusual extent and has claimed more victims, perhaps, than any other epidemic in a score of years. The germ has eluded the bacteriologists and medical men now agree that the best cure is prevention.

Scientific officials recognize that the influenza had spread throughout the world, *Salt Lake Tribune*, 12 November 1918, page 13.

Wednesday, 13 November 1918—Weather:

Stayed home all P.M. The Huns are evacuating Belgium, Alcase Lorraine and parts of Germany. The flu ban is still tight and seems the expidemic is getting worse since the grand celebration. Letter from Pete.

Thursday, 14 November 1918—Weather:

The Huns have violated the armistice by damaging property as they leave Belgium. Slim and Mr. Hackalo came for the evening. We had a glamdorius time. We learned to play poker. It is not neccessary to use wheat flour substitutes from now on. The sugar rations will also go soon.

Friday, 15 November 1918—Weather:

Nothing interesting at home or anywhere in town. Letter from Pete.

Saturday, 16 November 1918—Weather:

I wish something dashing would execute. Hal & Lauretta have been with us for one week. They are looking for a house.

Sunday, 17 November 1918—Weather: [See below]

The two Vivians came in late afternoon. We went walking in evening. A beautiful night, and not cold.

Monday, 18 November—Weather:

Spent noon with Viv taking pictures at [Mormon] Temple ground. Met a jolly good fellow named Miller.

Tuesday, 19 November 1918—Weather:

Nothing dashing today[129] The boys are on their way to Berlin. Oh! What a wonderful march. Wish I was with them.

Wednesday, 20 November 1918—Weather

Many of the boys will be home by New Years day.

Thursday, 21 November 1918—Weather: (see below)

Getting colder.

Friday, 22 November 1918—Weather: (See below)

Coldest day & night this fall. A terrific blizzard.

Saturday, 23 November 1918—Weather:

Oh! Zooy. The Utah boys may be home in time for Christmas. What a wonderful day it will be. Thanks to God.

Sunday, 24 November—Weather:

Sundays now are the busiest day of all since we cannot go to church. Hal came for a while & we then had a good dinner alone. Hal & Lauretta are in a new house now.

Monday, 25 November 1918—Weather:

A letter came from Shorty Tolman & one from Sergt. Moreno. Moreno is an Indian as I suspected.

Tuesday, 26 November 1918—Weather:

This is my first day with Dodge Bros. Co[130]. I fear I don't like it. They treat me as an honored guest, but it is [too] quiet. I wish I could hear old Millar kids foot steps come banging along again for a change. Lunched with Laura & Vivian.

Wednesday, 27 November 1918—Weather:

Laura and I called on The Circstons. Walter is ill with lung trouble. We took him some violets and surely had a nice time but left early. Walter looked unusually nice. All dolled up and no where to go.

Thursday, 28 November 1918—Weather:

We all went to Hal's place for dinner. I never had a better one. Then we sang songs in the evening about the fireplace. A wonderful Thanksgiving indeed. But Oh you turkey. This is truely a beautiful Thanksgiving for peace. Best one I ever had.

Editor's note: It appears that the following entry was written as a single entry covering both days.

Friday-Saturday, 29-30 November 1918—Weather:

Germany has sent us an appeal for food. They are hoplessly dishonorable. They don't regret one particle of their terrible attrocities. The Belgians are singing praises to their deliverers and are wild with joy. The whole world is rejoycing over the end of this terrible war. But everyone realizes that unless Germany is made uterly helpless, she will start something over again. And for generations to come they shall be outcasts both socially and commercially.

12

DECEMBER
All Dolled Up with Some Place to Go

Editor's note: It appears that the following entry was written as a single entry covering both days.

Sunday-Monday, 1-2 December 1918—Weather:

Today is Fast Sunday[131] and we cannot go to church. At least we can fast. The flue is raging all over the world. The death toll of the U.S. civilian population alone is bet. 300,000 & 350,000. Worse than the war casualties. And there are also thousands of soldiers over here and there dying off like flies. The worse scorge in years. Fortunately we have escaped it. I hope Billy boy is OK. Received a company picture of Pete at Camp Lewis, Wash.

Tuesday, 3 December 1918—Weather: (See below)

A letter from Ozy Rands from the trenches in France. He says he is sending me a helmet. His letter was mailed before the signing of the Armistice. The weather is so warm.

Wednesday, 4 December 1918—Weather:

Germany's plea for food is just another trick to have the peace conditions slackened. Them women over there had the nerve to call us their sisters. The dirty crooks them![132] A letter from Clare.

Editor's note: It appears that the following entry was written as a single entry covering four days.

Thursday-Sunday, 5-8 December 1918—Weather:

Nothing dashing but the boys are marching, marching on to Berlin. A victory march, but prepaired for the worst. Germany is disorganized, but she is also very trecherous and tricky. I would like to be with the occupation army. Not very pleasant I must say but tryumphant. The good old "Stars and Stripes" are being flown in France, Belgium & in Germany where ever our wonderful fighters go. But they are waiting patiently to get back to the good old U.S.A. They write brave letters to us stay-at-homes, so we won't worry but they are going through hell and then some for us and a principle. And not a whimper from any of them. We thought brave men were a thing of the past, but never were there braver men than our galant American boys. The most wonderful stories of self-sacrifice for comrades or country are told. Viv & Bert came. Viv stayed for dinner & then we visited the Stewards for the evening, we had a pleasant visit. Bert's indented huzzy was there. He's not classy enough.

Monday, 9 December 1918—Weather: (See below)

Laura & I tramped our feet wet in the sloppy snow that is falling, buying Xmas gifts for Dad & Mother. There is nothing of importance to speak of as the town is dead from the Influenza. And we feel quite dead from lack of amusement.

Tuesday, 10 December 1918—Weather:

The Boys have reach the River Rhine in Germany. They doing the real watch on the Rhine now.

Wednesday, 11 December 1918—Weather:

I like my work a little better now tho I have a great deal of time for something to do. Mr. Dodge, my boss, is very nice to work for. He reminds me of Lawrence Woolley. No wonder I like him.

Thursday-Friday, 12-13 December 1918—Weather:

Peat writes very often and Ozy writes quite often too from France. He has sent me a German helmet. I can hardly wait for it to come. The Indian Sergeant writes often too and so does Shorty. Jesse Evans wrote of his experiences in Paris on Peace day. The French people just about mauled the American boys to death. Showered them with flowers. He says "Alas, Sherman was strong." The girls kissed our boys just as if they had the right to. Ha! Ha!

On December 13, as part of the Army of Occupation, Oswin's unit was directed to cross the Rhine River at the Coblenz bridgehead (at the confluence of the Rhine River and the Moselle River), and continue its march to occupy the districts of Mayen, Ahrweiler, Adenau, and Cochem.

Coblenz in 1919; Koblenz, in the map below

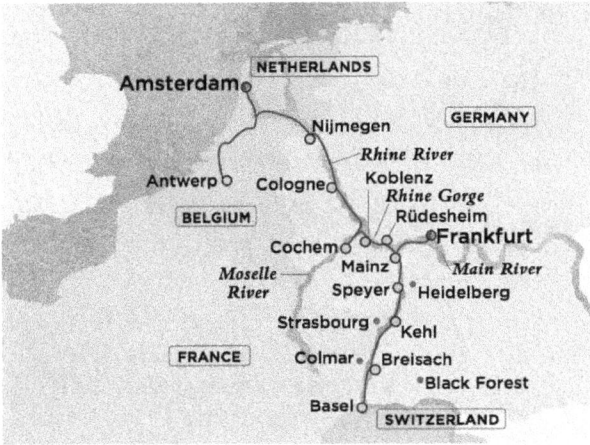

Map of Europe showing Koblenz at the confluence of the Rhine and Moselle rivers.

Saturday, 14 December 1918—Weather:

Hurried home & sewed. Nothing dashing.

Sunday, 15 December 1918—Weather:

Hal & Lauretta came. We had a delightful day. The soldier boys are being discharged very quickly and the town is full of them from all parts of the Union & some from Overseas.

HOME FROM FRANCE.

Big liners and transports bringing soldiers from France are arriving at the Atlantic ports almost every day, and there is rejoicing all over the land. Some of the men will be able to celebrate Christmas with their families, and their presence will bring more joy to the festive board. Thousands of others will be upon the high seas during the Yuletide season, while there will be hundreds of thousands more in France and Germany. Some have been designated for early return to this country, but the bulk of the American troops will remain until the peace treaty is signed.

Reports of shiploads of soldiers arriving at eastern ports and many on their way, *Salt Lake Tribune*, 19 December 1918, page 6.

Monday, 16 December 1918—Weather:

Laura & I mailed a large box of candy that we made yesterday. About two & a half pound to Lang and the same to Peterson. That ought to keep them from getting lonely for a while anyhow. They are so anxious to get home. Poor wolopers[133]. Sad but true.

Tuesday, 17 December 1918—Weather:

Oh! Zooey! Only a few more days before Xmas. We are considering a change in our home but at present I am not at liberty to speak more of it.

Wednesday, 18 December 1918—Weather:

All I do is sew, sew, sew.

Thursday, 19 December 1918—Weather:

The flu ban is up for theaters & churches[134] but I shall continue to remain away for some time as there is a great deal of flu yet all over.

SOCIETY

Twenty Guests at Luncheon for Visitor

A N attractively appointed luncheon was given by Mrs. William E. Day at her home, 2480 Fifth East street, yesterday in compliment to her sister, Miss Elizabeth King of Dayton, Ohio, who has been her guest for some time.

The Salt Lake Tribune reports a dozen society luncheons and meetings, 19 December 1918, page 4.

Friday, 20 December 1918—Weather:

I wrote Christmas cards to everyone out of town. Oh! But Xmas is a nuisance but a real pleasure.

Times Compares Influenza With Famous Plague

The 1918 influenza is compared to the Black Plague,
Salt Lake Herald-Republican,
20 December 1918, page 1.

LONDON, via Montreal, Dec. 19.— The Times medical correspondent says that it seems reasonable to believe that throughout the world about 6,000,000 persons perished from influenza and pneumonia during the past three months.

It has been estimated that the war caused the death of 20,000,000 persons in four and a half years. Thus, the correspondent points out, influenza has proved itself five times deadlier than war because in the same period, at its epidemic rate, influenza would have killed 100,000,000.

Never since the black death has such a plague swept over the world, he said, adding that the need of a new survey of public health measures have never been more forcibly illustrated.

Saturday, 21 December 1918—Weather:

Home early again. Nothing much.

Sunday, 22 December 1918—Weather:

Vivan K., Bert, & we girls had a tea party and we also pulled some fine taffy. Had a jolly time.

Monday, 23 December 1918—Weather:

Very busy prepairing for Xmas. Finished Blanches dress.

Tuesday, 24 December 1918—Weather:

This is Christmas eve & I worked more than ever selling vacuums. Laura worked till ten P.M. The flu ban is entirely lifted tonight but we are too busy to go out as yet. Tonight the misteries begin. Merry Xmas.

Wednesday, 25 December 1918—Weather: A beautiful Christmas. No snow.

Santa treated us finery. We had many callers and gifts. Johny Smith and Byron Turner U.S.N. who is here on furlough called. Had a nice chat. Dined at home the "By" called & we all visited Hal & Lauretta. Had a delightful Xmas. To bed at 12:30 [A.M.] Nothing to do till tomorrow.

Thursday, 26 December 1918—Weather:

Back to work again and sleepy as ever. Laura received a beautiful lovalier[135] of several golds and very delicate workmanship, set with saphires from Carl Atherton. A real surprise. I wonder why he sent it as he never seemed to care much.

Friday, 27 December 1918—Weather:

I visited Mr. & Mrs. Merrill after work. They always are so gracious to me & it seemed like the good old days. They walked home with me and Alta & Eunice Woodruff were at our house from Smithfield[136]. They are swell old pals.

Saturday, 28 December 1918—Weather:

In the evening we rushed like mad men and went to the Pantages theatre. We ate Walter's chocolates while there. Le Woodruff met us after and we went to the Odeon to dance. Had a jolly time even though [knew] a very few. I met a nice S.L. soldier, Mr. Boldin.

The program at the Pantages
for 28 December 1918.

And the review that caused so much
interest, *Salt Lake Herald-Republican*,
26 December 1918, page 4.

Sunday, 29 December 1918—Weather: Beautiful & cold.

Laura & I went with Le, Alta & Eunice to visit Hal and Lauretta. Had a
wonderful dinner & they left at five thirty for their train home. Laura & I
wanted to go skating but the fire place was too perswasive. Mr. Chambers
phoned while we were gone.

Monday, 30 December 1918—Weather:

Back again to work. I don't like it a bit for I get so lonely. But I must not
be so easily discouraged. I made my New Year resolution some time ago.
I believe I am a little teeny weeny bit better already but much more cavity
for improvement Anna. Get busy.

Tuesday, 31 December 1918 —Weather:

This is New Years Eve. By T. came for Laura. Daughters invited me out with them to help entertain a soldier boy but I had my date with Hal & Lauretta to go to the Odeon. I almost cried for I thought I was sluffed for they were late in coming. So out we started at last. We were all dolled up with some place to go. Violet pined on us and "everything." I met a nice Mr. Barnes of Fort D. He has peculiar black hair. Then I met Mr. Madsen who is twice as old as me. Then we with him went to the [Auditorium][137] then to the Newhouse Hotel grill room[138]. A wonderful night. Mr. Madsen showed me marked attention.

SPEAK EARLY! SPEAK EARLY!

Say right now how many places you want tonight at the big

New Year's Eve Supper

It'll be one of the delightful features of the fastest, merriest New Year's celebration you ever mixed in. Served from 9 p. m. to 1 a. m. $5 a plate, including covert charge.

Dashing Victory Revue

will be at its best and you can jazz until the wee small hours to the music of the finest jazz aggregation in town.

Table d'Hote Dinner Every Evening

We are serving an exceptionally, well-appointed and delicious table d'hote dinner every evening from 7 to 9, for $1.25 a plate, including covert charge.

Newhouse Hotel

Enjoy the Victory Revue while dining! It plays every evening from 7 to 9 and 10 to 12.30.

Dinner at the Newhouse Grill Room, *Salt Lake Herald-Republican*, 31 December 1918, page 3.

Anna's Notes for 1919

That is my record for 1918. Nothing much gained. Only the same place where I was before. Today my thoughts are with some one some where but I know not that place. I hope I have made a good impression on "him." But I admit that if he was to treat me beautifully I should not care. But as long as he don't care for me I am in hopes of meeting him again very soon. I am very imaginative and allow my thoughts to sore to dizzy heights, but still my sceptical part allows no bitter dissapointments. Here's hoping for better.

POSTSCRIPT

Sometime during the final month before the Armistice, the 107th Ammunition Train was loaned to the 88th Division, and then returned to the 32nd Division on 11 January. The 32nd Division in Germany was part of the Army of Occupation until April 1919.

Close examination of the photo below shows that Oswin's shoulder patch is that of the 32nd Division—the straight Red Arrow.

The Straight Red Arrow shoulder patch for the 32nd Division.

Corporal Oswin P. Rands in Germany as part of the Army of Occupation.

The 107th Ammunition Train was billeted in the town of Heimbach during its time in Germany. The town was a very small town near the border with Belgium and France. The "train" arrived at Heimbach on 18 January 1919 and departed on 20 March 1919. Perhaps the above photo was taken in Heimbach, although the troops had plenty of time to visit other areas in the vicinity.

In the logbook *Thru the War with Our Outfit,* John C. Acker describes the time being billeted in the homes of local German families in Heimbach as being very comfortable, with the hosts being very accommodating, and feeding the Americans extremely well.

Modern-day Heimbach in the Eifel mountains east of the Rhine River.

Departing from Heimbach, they traveled by boxcar across France, arriving at the port of Brest on 22 April 1919.

Oswin Rands departed from Brest, France, aboard the USS *Louisiana*[139] on 1 May 1919, and arrived back in the United States 13 May 1919 at Hoboken, New Jersey. The trip home was described as "wretched weather for our trip with the exception of but two days."

The passenger list indicated the unit was to be sent to Camp Merritt, New Jersey, where most of the returning troops were brought before their discharge. The camp had been under construction in December 1917 when Oswin departed for France.

The USS *Louisiana,* the ship that brought the 107th Ammunition Train home to America.

Soldiers disembarking at Hoboken piers at the end of WWI.

According to the *Rexburg Standard*, Oswin arrived home in Rexburg during the week of 19 June 1919.

Oswin Rands, son of Mr. and Mrs. H. Rands, returned home from overseas the latter part of the week. Mr. Rands spent several hard months in France, the latter part of the time being spent in Germany.

Corporal Oswin Rands arrives at home after several hard months in France and with the Army of Occupation in Germany, *Rexburg Standard*, 19 Jun 1919, page 1.

On 15 January 1920, the U.S. Census was taken at 1066 Emerson Avenue, where Anna's family lived.

The 1920 US Census for the Lund familly at 1066 Emerson Ave.

The 1920 U.S. Census at Salt Lake City for the Lund Family at 1066 Emerson Street

Billy was home from the Navy. Anna, Laura, Violet, and Don were at home. Anna was listed as working as a stenographer for an automobile company. In Anna's scrapbook is a photograph of four individuals, one of them Anna, in front of an automobile service company on which she wrote, "My first job after Business College at $75.00 per month at General Auto Service in Salt Lake City, Utah." The address is 115 East First South, Salt Lake City, approximately where Harmon's Grocery-City Creek is today.

On 10 January 1920, the U.S. Census was taken at Rockwell Aviation Field at San Diego, California, where Oswin Rands was listed as a 24-year-old Army private from Idaho. I have yet to find where Oswin went between his arrival in Rexburg in June 1919 and his posting at the aviation field on Rockwell Island in San Diego. I find no sign of him re-enlisting in the Army or having not yet been discharged. If his service record ever appears, perhaps the circumstances that had him still in the Army will become apparent.

Addresses at the Back of the Diary

(The date indicates the first occurance in 1918 of the name)

Miss Alta Woodruff, Box 825 Smithfield, Utah—27 December

Sergent John Chapla Co. F, 43rd Infantry, Camp Pike, Arkansas. Now Savannah, Georgia—(Married now.)—8 January

Private Robert J Mead Co. G, 42nd Infantry, Camp Dodge, Iowa (Moved to River guard at N.Y. Now at Mass. July 23, 1918—6 February)

Winnifred McWilliams, Wa 3758J—6 April

Shirley Stewart, 16th Co., C. A. C. of S. F. Ft Barry, Calif. (I could love you Shirley. Now I don't think so.),—6 June

Wag. Oswin P. Rands Hdgs. Co. 146 Machine Gun. Batt. Am. E. F. France. AM. P.O. 727—29 March

Mr. Joseph Evans Rexburg, Idaho Box 42 (The dearest brotherish cousin I have.) [Joseph's mother, Annie Maria Partington, was Anna's mother's sister]—10 June

Mr. Clearance Peterson Logan, Utah (He's nice but a blond)—31 January

Wm. E. Lund [Billy] c/o Postmaster of N.Y. U.S.S. *Pittsburgh*[140]. (my sailor brother, Bill[141])

Edward E. Curtis Co. 46 C. A. C. N. A. Presidio of S. F., California (he's funny)—20 June

Anna's Personal Notes

Had tonsils removed by Dr. Benneton Sat. Dec. 29, 1917. Bill for $35. Paid $5.00 on acct. on same day.

Started night school at Heneger's Business College on Nov. 19, 1917. Paid $5.00 for one month.

List of Names in the Diary and Commentary

(In alphabetical order with date of the first occurrence)

Note: Any reader who can add information about Anna's friends is invited to share them with me. Please contact me at rrands@earthlink.net.

Allan, Mr. – 1 March 1918

Mr Allan was only mentioned once, and Anna says only that she saw him at a ward dance. There are no further clues.

Andrews, Private Horace – 5 June 1918

"Viv & I met Corp. Newton Rains & Privt. Horace Andrews of B Co. 20 Inf." I cannot find a complete roster of B Company of the 20th Infantry at Fort Douglas. I see no possible candidates without more details.

Atherton, Carl – 18 January 1918

Anna does not specify any details about Carl Atherton except that he was honorably discharged for tuberculosis between January 27 and 29. A search of WWI draft registration records reveals an entry for a Carl Marion Atherton. He registered twice—once in Idaho Falls, Idaho, on 5 June 1917, and indicated that he was seventeen years old—too young to serve. The second registration, in San Francisco, California, is undated, but says he was 23 years old. This suggests that the second registration took place after 10 September, when he had passed another birthday. But this is a helpful discovery in that the reverse side identifies the date of Carl's discharge, January 28, and his infantry unit, the 20th Infantry—one of the regiments assigned to Fort Douglas.

In September 1919, Carl Marion Atherton applied for a job with the Northern Pacific Railway and denied any physical ailment that might render him unfit for railroad service. He was still working for the railroad well into the 1960s and living in Covina, (east of) Los Angeles, California. A Find-A-Grave entry for Carl Marion Atherton born on 10 September 1897 in Missouri, and reportedly died in Los Angeles County on 4 November 1985. If this is Anna's friend Carl Atherton, he certainly outlived his tuberculosis.

Barnes, Mr. – 31 December 1918

"I met a nice Mr. Barnes of Fort D. He has peculiar black hair." This is a peculiar comment about a man leading to the suggestion that he was a Black man, but there are no mentions of a Pioneer Battalion (a Black battalion) at Fort Douglas. When orders were issued for the demobilization of the Student Army Training Corps at the University of Utah, a man named Barnes was serving as a platoon leader. It is not clear when the unit was discharged. There are several thousand Barneses in the V.A. Master List, so without more details, this is a dead end.

Bennett, Dr Wilford W.

"Had tonsils removed by Dr. Benneton Sat. Dec. 29, 1917. Bill for $35. Paid $5.00 on acct. on same day." The records do not include a Dr. Benneton, but the City Directory contains a Dr. Wilford W Bennett who is an eye, ears, nose and throat physician.

Berg, Mr. & Mrs. – 22 September 1918

"Mr. & Mrs. Berg called and made us late for church." Arriving at the Lunds' home early Sunday morning suggests this couple didn't travel far to get there. There were about a dozen Berg families in the city directory for 1918, but the closest couple to the Lunds was Charles and Josephine Berg, who resided at 321 Hampton Street, about a half-mile away.

Bert – 4 February 1918

"Lunched with Bert & Isabell Steward & Vivian." It would seem that Bert and Isabell were a couple, but when Bert has an appendectomy in March, we discover that Bert is a she. So it appears that Bert and Isabell Steward may not be related. (See Isabell's entry below) When Bert is in the hospital, Anna and her friend Vivian visit her twice, which leads me to assume she is a fairly close friend. Nearly every time Bert appears in the diary, it is associated with Vivian. A couple of the times she drops in on the Lunds as if she lives nearby. Bert might have been a nickname for Alberta or Bertha, but without a surname it is a challenge to identify who Bert might be. I checked all the names in Anna's eighth grade graduating class at Emerson School and found a Bertha Violet Vunder, but this girl was married in 1915, and is unlikely to have been a part of Anna's social circle in 1918.

Beverley, Mr. – 5 January 1918

"Met some nice fellows among whom were Mess [sergeant] Emerson, Mr. Beverley a dandy boy & a funny jolly Dutchman named Franklin"

Birch, Miss – 30 April 1918

After a run-in with Mack, who was in trouble, Anna says she later spoke with Miss Birch and "that was sufficient." It is possible that Mack had fled from some trouble he was in and that Anna had turned him in by notifying Miss Birch. Or she had become fed up with him and complained to Miss Birch, who would be able to prevent him from bothering her anymore. In any case, the identity of Miss Birch is quite elusive without our knowing what kind of trouble Mack was in. One possible Miss Birch would be Flora Birch, who was a nurse, and whose family resided on the same block of Emerson Avenue that Anna lived on. Flora resided there with two sisters and their widowed mother, Amelia. In June, Flora, a recent University graduate, volunteered for government nursing service (Red Cross). A second possibility was Miss Charlotta Birch, a teacher at the University Training School, where some soldiers were attending military training classes.

Blanche – 23 December 1918

"Finished Blanches dress." The diary contains no clue about a Blanche who ordered a dress from Anna. The city directory lists about 100 Blanches, none of whom have a surname similar to one already mentioned in the diary.

Boldin, Mr. – 28 December 1918

"I met a nice S.L. soldier, Mr. Boldin." Assuming "S.L. soldier" meant a soldier from Salt Lake City, I searched for such a name in the Utah WWI military records with no success. There was a soldier named Rufus Bolton, but he died in France in September of influenza. The WWI V.A. Master Index yielded a dozen Boltons, but none were from Utah. Without further information, this is another dead end.

Braithwaite, Fred – 15 September 1918

"We entertained three University training soldier boys at dinner and home. We all had a great time. Mr. Frank T Carson, Corp. Wm. Jones, and Mr. Fred Braithwaite." Mr. Fred L Braithwaite was from Manti, Utah, and born on 12 February 1897. He was assigned to the Student Army Training Corps at the University of Utah until 29 October, when he was assigned to the 49th Artillery of the Coast Artillery Corps at Ft. Winfield Scott at San Francisco, California.

Brimsike or Brinnicke, Mr. – 10 February 1918

Given that Anna spelled this person's name two different ways suggests that neither spelling might be correct. A search of the city directory, newspapers, and census records for various alternative spellings does not reveal anything similar.

Byerline, Ada D. and Adalaide – 3 January 1918

Anna is sewing dresses for both Ada and Adeline. Ada and Albert

DeLos Byerline and their four children lived a few blocks from the Lunds. Albert was a foreman of carriers at the post office, possibly at the office where Ann'a father worked. Fern and Adalaide were daughters who were sixteen and fourteen, respectively, in 1918. Albert was born in Illinois in 1876, and Ada was born in England in 1878; they were married in Illinois.

Carson, Frank – 15 September 1918

"We entertained three University training soldier boys at dinner and home. We all had a great time. Mr. Frank T Carson, Corp. Wm. Jones, and Mr. Fred Braithwaite." Mr. Frank Carson was from Junction, Utah, a small town in the south-central part of Utah with a population of about 400 in 1918. His draft registration indicates he was born on 14 April 1897.

Cederholme, Ed – 28 May 1918

"Sherman and Ed Cederholme called on their machines." It is likely that these two men were soldiers who had access to motorcycles. Automobiles were often referred to as machines, but the context in this case is more likely to be motorcycles. The two men returned on 3 June to take Anna and her sister out riding. With so few details, I have not found a likely candidate for this person.

Chambers, Mr. – 10 November 1918

"Le & Ruby & Max came to dinner. Also Slim, Mr. Chambers and Mr. Nejadly." After a concerted effort to locate a soldier named Chambers who would be assigned to Fort Douglas, I have to say this is a dead end.

Chapla, Sergeant John – 8 January 1918

Sergeant John Chapla, of Co. F, 43rd Infantry, Camp Pike, Arkansas [now Savannah, Georgia], was Anna's current number one boyfriend. In Anna's scrapbook there is an undated photo of the two of them together. John is one of the few individuals whose details are listed in the address section of the diary. There is no evidence as to how they met or knew each other, but since it is early in the diary, I assume they met by 1917 and that he was in the military when they met, and probably that he was stationed at Fort Douglas before being transferred to Camp Pike. The 43rd Infantry Regiment was formed in June 1917 at Fort Douglas, Utah, which might explain how Anna met John. In the photo I can make out the sergeant stripes on his right sleeve, but the patch on his left sleeve is not clear. It is possible that he was at Fort Douglas because of serving in the Mexican Border clashes of 1915–16. Fort Pike was the home of the 87th Infantry. Camp Pike was never transferred to Savannah, Georgia, so I suppose that Sergeant Chapla was discharged and resided in Savannah.

Anna spells the sergeant's name two different ways; on the photo it is Capla, and in the diary it is Chapla. However, the name Chapla appears in many records to be an anglicized version of the Polish name Czapla. I found an article in the Salt Lake Tribune for 5 July 1917 announcing promotions for the 43rd Infantry regiment. The story indicates that Private John Czapla has been promoted to Corporal.

It was announced in October, 1917, that the 43rd Infantry was transferred to Fort Pike, Arkansas.

Further descriptions of the two infantry units make it sound as if the first soldiers that were put in the two units were from the 2nd Infantry that saw action in the 1916–1917 border clashes with Mexico. These details correspond to my earlier thoughts.

Anna receives a letter from John on 4 April 1918 announcing his marriage. She had suspected something was going on since he had not written for a while. John's V.A. Master Index record indicates he was born 4 February 1890 and died 26 Jul 1932, and that he enlisted 6 April 1917. The record contains an address at 536 E State St., Savannah, Georgia, but it is not clear when that address was in effect, although Anna wrote across his entry in the diary address page that John was now at Georgia. I do not find an entry in the 1930 Census in Georgia for him. There is an entry in the 1930 Census for John working as a welder in a hospital, with a note that his service in the military was in Mexico, but his wife was not with him.

Cerston/Cirston or Sirstin, Walter and Hertha – 5 July 1918

"Went to Lagoon with Pete, Laura & Walter & Hertha Cerstons." Hertha Sirstins was a 24-year-old German girl who worked as a clerk at Cohn's, a womens' major clothing store in downtown Salt Lake City, a place Anna probably frequented often and where Anna became familiar with the clerks. Walter was a salesman at Cohn's as well.

Chapman, Mr. – 1 May 1918

I assume Mr. Chapman is a soldier from Fort Douglas. But Chapman is a very common name.

Circston, Walter and Hertha – 27 November 1918

"Laura and I called on The Circstons. Walter is ill with lung trouble. We took him some violets." See Walter & Hertha Sirstins – 5 July.

Clever, Mr. – 6 January 1918

"Mr. Clever & Moore called on Laura & I in evening and we went to church." The reference by Mr. for both men suggests they were soldiers from Fort Douglas. Also, going to church suggests they might have been Mormons.

Mr. Clever is mentioned several more times in the diary, but never with a first name. Anna describes him as having "such beautiful teeth & hair as waivy & heavy as can be." I could not find any WWI draft cards for a Mr. Clever of an appropriate age born in Utah or a nearby state. His last reference in the diary is 3 February. There are hundreds of Clevers in the United States. However, if I were to guess at a possible candidate, it would be a man who registered for the draft in the western part of the country, which would lead to an assignment in a regiment being trained and mobilized at Fort Douglas. My choice would favor someone who would have a family tree in FamilySearch FamilyTree because that would increase his chances of being a Mormon. One such individual is Oscar Raymond

Clever, who was born in 1895 in Iowa, but who was single and residing in Fullerton, California, when he registered for the draft on 5 June, 1917, at the age of twenty-one. At this point I have no evidence that this is the man who called on Anna and her sister on the 6th of January, 1918. But for now, this is my best guess.

Collins, Frank – 12 March 1918

Anna's close friend Vivian introduced Frank to her, and he wanted to have a date with her. But Anna refused to accept a date without seeing him ahead of time. It is not clear if Frank is a soldier or not. Anna does not mention him again, suggesting that the two of them never met.

Curtis, Edward B. – 20 June 1918

"Received a letter...from Edward E. Curtis." Edward is listed in the address section of the diary with the following entry: "Edward E. Curtis Co. 46 C.A.C.N.A. Presidio of S. F., California," along with the comment that he was funny. According to records of the Coastal Artillery, the 46th Artillery was not constituted until July 1918 and activated until September in Virginia. In October it shipped out to France. If Edward was assigned to the Presidio of San Francisco, he would have been serving at Fort Scott. I cannot locate any records that verify his unit in June 1918.

Cushman, Earl – 1 September 1918

"We met Earl Cushman and Jesse Marryhue." It is my guess that Earl Cushman was not a soldier, because Anna met them in the park and went to a private party at their place on the west side of Salt Lake City. Fort Douglas was on the east side. Furthermore, Anna implies that they were younger than her, commenting that they reminded her of when she was seventeen. In the city directory, I found an entry for Earl Cushman residing at 447 3rd East—not on the west side.

Drot, Kate – 1 May 1918

I cannot find any references to a Kate or Katherine Drot or Drott in the city directory, newspapers, or census records. Kate was nowhere to be found. Perhaps Anna badly misspelled her surname. Kate appears on 5 May, and they attend Sunday meetings at the First Ward, suggesting that Kate may have been a member of the LDS church.

Edwards, Douglas – 28 February 1918

A letter arrives from this man on this date, and again in October. There are no further clues about him, other than in October he is on his way across the country to be shipped overseas to France—implying that he is a soldier. One highly plausible candidate is a John Douglass Edwards, who was Anna's first cousin from her mother's Partington line. He was from Logan, Utah, and was a private first class in the 5th Battalion, 62 Infantry. He was born 13 Aug 1894 and died 10 February1961. The regiment was organized in 1917 in California and assigned to the 15th Infantry Brigade, a component of the 8th Division at Camp Fremont, California. The regiment departed Camp Fremont on 18 October 1918, which corresponds to the date of his letter to Anna in October. They were headed for Camp Mills, New York, and then movement overseas to France. On 22 October 1918, the 62nd Regiment was detached from the 8th Division and remained at Camp Mills, New York.

Edwards , Uncle Ed – 6 October 1918

"Uncle Ed Edward came." This would be Anna's uncle Edward Edwards, the husband of Aunt Mary Emily Partington Edwards. The Edwards family was from Logan, Utah, and must have been visiting the Lunds in Salt Lake City.

Edwards, Margarete – 5 October 1918

Margarete was one of Anna's cousins from her mother's Partington side. She was the daughter of Anna's Aunt Mary Emily Partington Edwards, and would have been sixteen years old at this time.

Emerson, Mess Sergeant – 5 January 1918

"Met some nice fellows among whom were Mess [sergeant] Emerson, Mr. Beverley a dandy boy & a funny jolly Dutchman named Franklin"

Emma, Aunt – 1 August 1918

"Wrote a card to Aunt Emma in Logan." In the family records I have traced a Myrtle Emma Edwards, one of Anna's cousins from her mother's Partington line, who was living in Logan, Utah, about 80 miles north of Salt Lake City. Emma's mother, Emily, would have been her aunt. So its anyone's guess who Aunt Emma is.

Ernst, Billie and Peggy – 4 January 1918

Anna meets Billie on the street and accepts a luncheon invitation for the following Monday. Anna refers to their "sweet captivating jolly little girl 18 mo. old daughter."

The only William Ernst in any Salt Lake records is William Ernst, married to Virginia. If this is "Billie" he would have been 50 years old at the time and not likely to have an eighteen-month-old daughter. Peggy is short for Margaret, making it unlikely that Virginia is her name. I do not see a draft registration record that fits the family. I find no newspaper records that fit. Anna does not mention them anywhere else in her diary. Without more clues, this is likely to be a dead end.

Evans, Bessie – 26 July 1918

"Bessie Evans is visiting us from Idaho. I like [her] very much." Bessie was another of Anna's cousins from her mother's Partington line. She was the daughter of Alice Louisa Partington Evans and was born in 1900 in Rexburg, Idaho.

Eddy Evans and Sarah ("better half") – 8 June 1918

Edward Partington Evans one of Anna's cousins from her mother's

Partington line. He was born in 1898 in Idaho and had just married Sarah Cluff of Utah three days earlier in Salt Lake City. I suspect that all the Evans family members who were in town during this week were attending the wedding celebrations.

Evans, Jesse – 20 July 1918

"Card from Jesse Evans. He is going 'over there.'" Jesse was an older brother to Joseph Evans and one of Anna's cousins from her mother's sister on the Partington line. He was 26 years old, and served in the US Military postal service.

Evans, Joan and Edgar/Eddy ("better half") – 8 June 1918

"Then out to Saltair with Joan & Eddy Evans & their better halfs." Johannah "Joan" Evans was one of Anna's cousins from her mother's Partington line. She was born in 1896 in Rexburg, Idaho, and was married to Edgar Stanfield, who was born in Arkansas.

Evans, Joseph (cousin) – 7 June 1918

Joseph was the son of Anna's aunt Annie Marie Partington Evans, who lived in Rexburg, Idaho. He was born in July 1897, married in 1921, and died in February 1956 in Idaho Falls, Idaho. As Anna mentions, he was "deaf" (hearing impaired). He was close friends with Anna and her family.

Evans, Porky – 8 June 1918

The family records do not identify Porky, although it is likely that he was part of the Evans family from Rexburg, Idaho, that was visiting Anna's family in Salt Lake City. The only possible sibling of Joseph would have been David Lawrence Evans, born in 1880 and died in 1941. I cannot find any evidence that he was nicknamed Porky.

Franklin (Dutchman)– 5 January 1918

"Met some nice fellows among whom were Mess s[e]argent Emerson, Mr. Beverley a dandy boy & a funny jolly Dutchman named Franklin." Is Franklin a surname or a given game?

Genevie – 28 September 1918

"Genevie also went" to the Liberty Loan Auto parade. Too little detail to identify this person. My guess is that she is a neighbor girl, but without a surname, it's anybody's guess.

Grass, Edgar – 10 July 1918

"A letter from Edgar Grass." It is possible that this is the same person as Edgar B. Trass (See 22 June). Edgar Bauer Grass was a PFC in the 45th Artillery, a unit of the Coast Artillery Corps. His unit w as one of the few that were shipped to France. He was from Hays, Kansas. There is little chance to validate this assumption.

Grossen, Lewis – 17 April 1918

"Lewis Grossen and Mr. Senior called and spent the evening with the excuse of selling W.S. [War Savings] Bonds." The WWI draft registration records do not include a Louis or Lewis Grossen, nor do the V.A. Master Index records. The Utah birth records include a Louis Grossen born in Salt Lake City on 11 January 1901. He would have been seventeen years old in 1918—too young to join the military for WWI. This might explain why he was going to private residences to solicit W.S. Bond purchases. Were he or his partner already acquainted with the Lund family? He lived nearly two miles from the Lund residence. He married Mae Linnell Decker in 1922.

Hackalo, Mr. – 14 November 1918

"Slim and Mr. Hackalo came for the evening." William W. Hakalo from Glenrock, Wyoming, born 28 October 1897, is the only individual with that surname in the WWI Draft registration records. He does not appear in the V.A. Master index, nor in any newspapers for 1918.

Hansen, Ellen – 31 May 1918

"I went to night school and road home with Ellen Hansen." It is likely that Anna and Ellen rode home together on the trolley. The 1920 U.S. Census lists an Ellen Hansen, married to John Hansen and with two small children, living at 1748 9th East, about six blocks from Anna's house. She would have been about 28 years old. She was Norwegian, as was Anna's father, a strong possible connection.

Helton, Grant – 8 March 1918

Anna goes to a dance with her sister and Grant Helton. I suspect it was Anna's responsibility to act as a chaperone for her younger sister. During the evening, Anna sends a message to Mac (McGinnis) by way of Grant, which implies that Grant was a soldier at Fort Douglas and knew Mac. The name Helton was not common, so his name may have been Holton. There was a Grant Holton at Fort Douglas, although he was slightly older than Anna. This person was severely injured in May 1918 in France.

Indian, The – 12 December 1918

See Sergeant Moreno

Jack – 23 June 1918

"I met a nice fellow named Jack" at a concert in the park. No way to determine who Jack is.

Mrs. Joan and her husband – 14 April 1918

See Joan Stanfield.

Jones, Corp. William – 15 September 1918

"We entertained three University training soldier boys at dinner and home. We all had a great time. Mr. Frank T Carson, Corp. Wm. Jones, and Mr. Fred Braithwaite." The only William Jones from Utah I can locate who served in the Student Army Training Corps (SATC) in Salt Lake City is William L Jones from Cedar City, Utah. He was born 14 September 1897.

Kershaw – 6 September 1918

"Went joy riding with Kershaw and the girls." Too few details to determine who Kershaw was.

Kramer, Pvt. – 11 October 1918

"Pvt. Kramer of the 70th Engineers, Ft. Douglas, came for the evening." There are more than 4,000 entries in the V.A. Master index for individuals who served in WWI with the name Kramer. At this point, I tried to imagine why a soldier from Fort Douglas would have been invited to the Lund home for the evening, perhaps for dinner. My best guess is that he was from Salt Lake City and was known to the Lunds, and/or his family were from Norway and the local Norwegian community had a standing invitation for soldiers whose families were from Norway. There was only one entry in the list of Kramers at Fort Douglas who was from Utah, and that was Joseph Kramer, born 5 Dec 1886, who was from Salt Lake City, Utah. He was not Norwegian.

Kuhn, Vivian – 22 February 1918

Anna mentions sewing a dress for Vivian during the later part of February, and Vivian came over in October to pick one up, suggesting that Anna sewed more than one dress for her. It seems that Vivian was more than a dressmaking client, because she shows up in the diary multiple times without mention of a dress. Among all of the records I have searched there is one Vivian Kuhn who is listed in the eighth grade graduating class of 1916 of Uinta school, which would have made her born about 1903. Uinta School was about 1 mile away from Emerson School where Anna graduated a couple of years earlier. I am unable to identify her family.

Lafont, Harold A. (Superintendent) – 4 January 1918

Apparently Anna is serving as her Ward's Sunday School secretary and is responsible for handling the annual attendance report. It is curious that there are two superintendents, unless one of them is an assistant.

The first is probably Harold A. Lafount, (1880–1952), an Englishman who resided within a block of Anna's home at 1486 11th East.

Lang – 16 December 1918

"Laura & I mailed a large box of candy that we made yesterday. About two & a half pound to Lang and the same to Peterson." It sounds as though Anna shipped one large box containing two separate boxes for Lang and Peterson. If so, Lang and Peterson must have been in the same unit, which she implies was in France—she called them "wolopers" and said they were anxious to come home. I have no clue about Lang.

Larson, Mr. – 1 March 1918

Anna mentions that she saw Mr. Larson from Fort Douglas at a church dance. Earlier in the week, Anna mentions that she posted advertisements at the Soldiers Club regarding the dance on this evening, which suggests why Mr. Larson and Mr. Allan were there. This is the only mention of Mr. Larson or Mr. Allan in the diary, making it nearly impossible to identify either of them.

Larson, Sarah – 10 May 1918

"I received some motherly advise from an old school friend who was Sarah Larson. She is surely a married stiff." It's not clear if Larson is Sarah's maiden name or her married name. Since Anna has not been attending business classes for very long, her reference to "an old school friend" suggests that they were friends at Emerson Elementary School, however, there is no Sarah Larson listed along with Anna at the graduation ceremony. One possible candidate is a Sarah Larsen whose father, Olaf, was from Norway, and who was Anna's same age, and who resided at 1011 Wilson Ave., about one-half mile from Anna's home. She had only been married for about two weeks, not quite what one would think of as a "married stiff."

Lindow, Gotleib and wife – 24 March 1918

James Gottlieb Lindow, twenty-one, and Lilian Leona Allred, sixteen, were married 7 January. By the 1920 U.S. Census, the Lindows were living in Fresno, California. The 1920 Census in Salt Lake City shows a household at 1206 Bryan Ave, just a couple of blocks from Anna's house, that included both Wilsons and Lindows. When Anna takes a few minutes to visit the Wilsons and then says she meets Gotfried Lindow's wife, it seems plausible that she visited this household.

Lund, Hal, Lauretta, Allen, and Glenna – 14 August 1918

"Lauretta & little Allen & Glenna came from Denver." Lauretta is Anna's sister-in-law, wife of her oldest brother, Hal. Allen and Glenna were their three-year-old son and two-year-old daughter.

Le – 14 January 1918

See Leander Lund, Anna's older brother.

Lund, Leander (Le), Ruby, and Maxfield – 3 February 1918

Leander (Le) Lund and his wife, Ruby LaVern Frederickson, Anna's older brother and sister-in-law. Their son was six-month-old Maxfield Frederickson Lund.

Lund, Max – 13 January 1918

See Leander Lund, Anna's older brother.

Lund, Ruby – 13 January 1918

See Leander Lund, Anna's older brother.

Lund, William (Billy Boy) – 7 February 1918

Billy, Anna's brother who was serving on the USS *Pittsburgh*. Censorship made it so that Anna often did not know where his ship was deployed. At one point he was in Rio de Janeiro, Brazil; influenza had killed a large number of sailors aboard the ship.

Lunstrum – 2 March 1918

Anna and her sister Laura were invited to a house party at the Lunstroms/Lundstrums but declined the invitation. Several Lundstrom families were listed in the city directory, but none lived close to the Lund residence. One was a family with an eighteen-year-old son whose mother was born in Norway; they lived on Post Street. Their names were August, Valborg, and Eugene. Given Anna's father's Norwegian origins, this is possibly the family involved.

Mac or Mack – 8 March 1918

This is the first of many mentions of Mac. He has not been mentioned by his surname, and from here on out he is just Mac or Mack. Anna's relationship with Mac began at least nine months earlier and now in the diary is enigmatic. In Anna's scrapbook and in her writing fifty years later, several photographs show up referring to a "beau" she labels as McGinnis. She wrote, "He was Irish and a lot of fun. He was much older than I and treated me with the greatest respect" and "he begged me in all sincerity to marry him at Thanksgiving time." She has little good to say about him and claims at one point to discontinue ever seeing him again. Then he shows up again in her life, and she willingly allows him to court her. The next Sunday morning when he calls and she doesn't want her family to know about it shows her dilemma about how she plans to treat him and how she wants her family to treat him.

Madsen, Mr. – 31 December 1918

"Then I met Mr. Madsen who is twice as old as me. A wonderful night. Mr. Madsen showed me marked attention." Twice as old as Anna would make him 40 years old. I cannot locate a Mr. Madsen that fits this criterion.

Margetts, Mrs. – 14 July 1918

"Visited Mrs. Margetts." There are many individuals named Margetts in the city directory, but one very likely candidate would be Cacia Margetts, who was married to John Margetts and was living at 433 Emerson Ave, about 1.5 miles west on the same street as Anna's home. John and Cacia were married in February 1912 and were a young couple belonging to the same Mormon congregation.

Marryhue, Jesse – 1 September 1918

"We met Earl Cushman and Jesse Marryhue." It is my guess that Jesse Marryhue was not a soldier because Anna met the two men in the park and went to a private party at their place on the west side. Fort Douglas was on the east side. Furthermore, Anna implies that they were younger than she, commenting that they reminded her of when she was seventeen. The city directory had no entry for the name Jesse Marryhue or any variations.

Martin, Sergeant – 4 February 1918

Anna only says that she met Sergeant Martin, supposedly when she went to school on the evening of February 4. As Martin can be both a given name and a surname, identifying who this is was doubly challenging and impossible.

Maxon, Maxine – 9 October 1918

"Met my old school friend Maxine Maxon." The city directory lists Maxine Maxon residing at 2009 E. 2100 South, and her parents were Hal Y. Maxon, a schoolteacher, and Mrs. Maxon, a milliner.

McGinnis, Mac or Mack – 08 March 1918

See Mac

Mead, Robert J. – 6 February 1918

Private Robert J. Mead of Company G, 42nd Infantry, Camp Dodge, Iowa (Moved to River guard at New York, then at Massachusetts. July 23, 1918) was listed in the address section at the back of the diary. Anna wrote a half-dozen letters, some of which never reached him, so she sent one by registered mail. According to his V.A. Master Index listing, he was born 6 September 1894 and died 23 April 1966. He was discharged on 23 January1919 as a corporal. Robert married Mae Gaddis in 1925 in Sioux City, Iowa, and they farmed in South Dakota after their marriage. They had three children.

Merrill, Dorothy – 22 January 1918

Dorothy was a dear friend of fifteen-year-old Anna; she died on 17 March 1914 at LDS Hospital in Salt Lake City, Utah, of heart disease and pneumonia. Anna's scrapbook has a photo of Dorothy and a copy of the funeral description clipped from a newspaper with the source of the article missing. I have yet to locate the original newspaper source of the clipping. Dorothy was an older sister to Mildred, whose death is mentioned on 21 January 1918. Dorothy's funeral reveals that she was highly regarded in the community and that her family must have been well connected in Mormon leadership. Several high-ranking authorities of the church attended the funeral services, including two members of the Quorum of Twelve Apostles, and one future Apostle and member of the First Presidency.

Merrill, Mildred – 21 January 1918

The death certificate for Mildred Merrill indicates that she died of heart complications resulting from diphtheria at age seven. Her family lived on Harrison Avenue about six blocks from the Lunds. According to the Utah Public Health Association, many midwives unwittingly carried infections from one home to another. Diphtheria wiped out entire families with a death rate of 525 per 100,000. By 1920, a vaccination nearly eradicated diphtheria in the U.S. It is evident because of the names of the high ranking elders of the LDS Church who were speakers at the funeral services that the Merrill family was well placed in the LDS community in Salt Lake City.

Miller, Mr. – 18 November 1918

"Met a jolly good fellow named Miller." With a common name like Miller, it is unlikely that this man can be tracked down.

Moore, Mr. – 6 January 1918

As for Mr. Moore, he appears in the diary once more on 13 February. "We could hardly get away from Mr. Jack Moore & Mr. Cowel." For a guess regarding Mr. Moore, I would select John or Jack Beals Moore, who also registered in Fresno, California, on 5 June 1917 and was discharged on 6 Dec 1918. He also is listed in FamilySearch FamilyTree. I have no solid evidence that Jack Beals Moore is the soldier who called on Anna and her sister.

Moreno, Sergt. – 31 October 1918

"Yesterday a letter came from a Sergt. Moreno, a person unknown to me." When Sergeant Moreno writes a second time, Anna says he is an "Indian." His ethnicity might not have been Native American. Without more clues, this is a dead end.

Morgan, Mr. – 17 March 1918

Mr. Morgan appears in the diary on 20 Jan., along with Mr. Rowe, both of whom are of the 20th Infantry. No soldier in the available records named Morgan is listed.

Nejadly, Mr. – 10 November 1918

"Le & Ruby & Max came to dinner. Also Slim, Mr. Chambers and Mr. Nejadly." Ten individuals by the name Nejadly, or variations, appear on the V.A. Master Index, but none of them are listed among the units assigned to Fort Douglas. It may be that one of them was there temporarily.

Odbert, Mrs. – 29 July 1918

"Mrs. Odbert also came." Mrs. Lydia (Thomas) Odbert and her family lived down the street and around the corner on 11th East from Anna's house. I suspect she was one of Anna's dressmaking customers.

P., Viv – 27 October 1918

"Then in the evening Laura, Vivian and I went to Shultzs to see Viv P." The "Schultzs" are probably the Schultzes, first mentioned on 10 July in conjunction with Viv and her cousins. Without knowing Anna's relationship to the Schultzes and her full surname, we have not identified Viv.

Palmer, Myrtle – 29 May 1918

"Then went to Myrtle Palmer's for P.M." After serving near downtown at a train depot, Anna drops by Myrtle Palmer's home. In the 1917 city directory, there is a Myrtle H Palmer residing at 648 Elizabeth Ave, which would have been near the trolley car lines on the way home from the train depot. Myrtle was the nineteen-year-old daughter of Thomas and Lillie Palmer and worked as a clerk for Cohn's, a downtown business.

Parker, Marie – 28 April 1918

"After which we went to Parker's store. Mrs. Parker is just dandy." Probably the Liberty Park Grocery Store at 679 East 9th South run by Marie and William Parker. The Parkers were not listed in the 1919 or 1920 city directories.

Paul, George – 10 February 1918

Anna mentions on this date that one of her father's friends, Mr. George Paul, visited the Lunds and stayed for dinner, and "Mr. Paul told some of his must unusual experiences in South America." On February 23 Anna saw Mr. Paul and Mr. Brinnicke, seemingly when she was on her way to work, at work, or on her way home from work. The fact that Anna met Mr. Paul and Mr. Brimsike together nearly two weeks apart suggests they could have been associates in business or friends. In the 1920 U.S. Census, a 33-year-old George M Paul is listed as born in Germany and married to twenty-year-old Ebba, with a twenty-month-old daughter, Rose Mary. They lived on McClelland St. but closer to downtown, about three miles away.

Peat – 12-13 December 1918

"Peat writes very often." This may be a misspelled reference to Clarence Peterson, who had been sent to Ft. Lewis, Washington, and apparently was in France at the time of the Armistice.

Coleman Perkins, Alabama Slim – 3 October 1918

"The most interesting Southerner who can tell great stories called on us with his friend,... 'Alabama Slim' Coleman Perkins and Mr. Whitaker." The only person in the V.A. Master Index named Coleman Perkins from Alabama is Coleman Kingman Perkins from McKinley, Alabama, born 1 April 1893. He enlisted on 5 September 1918, which means he ended up at Fort Douglas very soon thereafter.

Pete – 5 July 1918

Pete is mentioned several times in the diary but without any clues about him. It is safe to say he was a soldier who left about this time for some other place. It is possible this is Clarence Petersen.

Peterson, Clarence – 31 January 1918

Sometimes misspelled as Clearance. "I was extremely surprised by a letter from Mr. Clearence Peterson who is in Ogden. He wishes to become better a[c]quainted if not in person by writing." This is an intriguing entry, but multiple Clarence Petersons were listed in Ogden's city directory. However, Anna includes Clearance Peterson among the names on the address page at the back of her diary. There she lists his address as Logan, Utah. Anna's mother has family connection in Logan. Anna receives another letter from Clarence on 15 February and again on 25 April, in Logan. On 18 May he writes and includes a photo prompting her to say, "[H]e is very nice looking." She writes a letter to him on 20 June. Then, on 4 July, he shows up at Anna's house having come all the way from Idaho to see her—no clue where in Idaho. They have lunch together the next day. Then she receives another letter on 16 September but declares "he don't count any more. The only time he writes is when there is no one else or nothing else." He writes again on 31 October and now she says she likes his "stile." Finally, on 16 December, Anna sends 2½ pounds of homemade candy to him. The only other clue she gives is that he is blond. She says he is "nice but a blond." There is a Clarence A. Peterson born in Logan, 12 July 1900, who was blond, but there is no draft registration or V.A. Master Index record for him.

Pickett, Jean – 3 February 1918

Brother Pickett was probably a member of Anna's same LDS Ward. It was undoubtedly little two-year-old Jean Pickett whose funeral Anna attended. She had been under a doctor's care since 10 January.

Jean died of bronchopneumonia; the family lived at 1307 McClellan St. which was about a half-mile from the Lund home.

Quinn, Jack – 31 August 1918

"Received a card from Jack Quinn. He is soon to go "over there." Not enough details to distinguish this fellow from the famous baseball pitcher, Jack Quinn, or from the five other J. Quinns in V.A. Master Index from Utah.

R., Ruth – 1 May 1918

Ruth R shows up on this date with a Mr. Chapman and friend. This is the only reference to these individuals.

Radabaugh, Evelyn Paramore – 17 March 1918

Evelyn and her family lived around the corner and partway down Roosevelt Street. It is likely she was a childhood friend. She was two years older than Anna and had married a soldier, Earl V Radabaugh, from Ohio, in December 1917. The marriage took place in Iowa. Earl was a soldier in the 42nd Division at Fort Douglas.

Rains, Corp. Newton – 5 June 1918

"Viv & I met Corp. Newton Rains & Privt. Horace Andrews of B Co. 20 Inf." I cannot find a complete roster of B Company of the 20th Infantry at Fort Douglas. The only probable candidate that fits Corp. Newton Rains is a Cpl. Ivey Newton Ranes from Georgia, who enlisted on 12 December 1917 and was assigned to the Student Army Training Corps (SATC). He was discharged in December 1918, never seeing service in France. He was born on 3 October 1895. A group of SATC soldiers was training at the University of Utah, and perhaps this man was part of that group.

Ramsey, Dr. – 29 April 1918

Two dentists named Ramsey were listed in the 1918 city directory for Salt Lake City: Dr. Charles A. Ramsey at 400 Scott Bldg. 168 South Main, and Dr. Roy H Ramsey at 113 South Main. Both offices were within a block or two around the corner from Dr. Tripp's office. Dr. Charles A. Ramsey was the closer.

Rands, Oswin – 29 March 1918

Oswin Percival Rands became my grandfather after Anna married him in 1921 and they had children. He was from Rexburg, Idaho, but after the war he eventually moved to Salt Lake City. See Grandpa Dutch in the Prologue.

Roberts, B. H. – 24 July 1918

"B.H. Roberts spoke." Brigham H. Roberts was a popular speaker and later a General Authority of the Mormon Church. At the time he was a lieutenant and chaplain in the U.S. Army. He published one of the popular histories of the church.

Rowe, Mr. – 20 January 1918

Mr. Rowe is first mentioned in the diary along with Carl Atherton, but eventually shows up on his own or with other soldiers. Anna is infatuated with Mr. Rowe and says in June, "I am in love with Mr. Rowe. But he is in love with someone else. Well thats always my luck. Gee! but I think he is grand." Because he appears in the diary two days after Carl Atherton wants to introduce his friend, a sheep herder, it is highly possible that Mr. Rowe is the sheep herder friend, and that he is also assigned to the 20th Infantry along with Atherton. He is also mentioned much later with a Mr. Morgan who is also with the 20th Infantry. I have yet to locate any other possible clue.

Schultze – 10 July 1918

"Visited Schultez's & Viv's cousins on the way [home]." There are several variations of the spelling for this name with many people listed in the 1918 city directory. One possible candidate would be Anna Schultze, who was a dressmaker living east of the downtown area.

Senior, Mr. – 17 April 1918

Mr. Senior appears at Anna's house along with Lewis Grossen, which raises some questions. Since Anna refers to him as "Mr." similarly to the way she refers to soldiers, is he accompanying Louis as a member of the military? Or is he another member of the Salt Lake City war bond committee working the community for war bond sales? And is he the same age as Louis, or older? One possible individual might be Clair Senior, born 8 April 1901 in Salt Lake City, the son of Edwin Williams Senior, an attorney, residing at 1530 Indiana Ave. Clair Senior married Sarah Lillian Worlton in 1927 at Stanford, California. It is unlikely I will be able to confirm this possibility.

Shorty – 2 September 1918

It is likely this "Shorty" is Rufus Tolman. See 3 August 1918.

Sirstins or Cirstons/Cerstons, Walter and Hertha – 5 July 1918

"Went to Lagoon with Pete, Laura & Walter & Hertha Cerstons." Hertha Sirstins was a 24-year-old German woman who worked as a clerk at Cohn's, a women's clothing store in downtown Salt Lake City, a place Anna probably frequented often and where Anna became familiar with the clerks. Walter was a salesman at Cohn's as well.

Slim, Alabama – 3 October 1918

See Coleman Perkins.

Smith, Johnny – 25 January 1918

"Joh[n]ny Smith was there (at the church dance). Good to see him again." There is no indication that John Smith was in the military, nor when or where Anna had last encountered him. Since he was at the ward dance, it is possible that he was LDS but had not been attending Anna's ward for a period of time. John Smith called on the Lund family on Christmas

Day, along with a friend in the Navy, but Smith is such a common name, especially in the LDS church, it is unlikely that I can pinpoint who he is.

Smith, Maud and June – 2 September 1918

"Maud & June Smith & others visited us." There is a Smith family living at 843 Arapahoe St., about four miles west of the Lund home, consisting of William H Smith married to Elizabeth Ann Partington with two daughters, Maud and Junia. They were Anna's cousins.

Spencer, Marva – 16 March 1918

Anna meets Marva at a women's clothing store. Her diary entry is, "I met Marva Spencer at Walker's. Gee, but I like her. I hope I can know her better.". There are no clues about when and where she first meets her. Anna mentions visiting her a couple of more times in the next couple of months. On one occasion, she visits with Winnie and Marva. A newspaper article from early February mentions girls being involved in collecting small change on the streets for the war fund-raising efforts, with each girl sponsored by a business in Salt Lake City. One of the girls sponsored by Walkers Bros. women's clothing store is Marva Spencer. Anna would have spent considerable time at Walkers, and if Marva was a clerk at the store, she would likely have encountered her. Another newspaper article on 28 February mentions a Miss Marva Spencer of 1229 Bryan Ave. being involved as a successful recruiter of enlisted men on the streets of the city ("Salt Lake Joan of Arc Arouses Men Patriotism, Salt Lake Telegram"). The address is less than a half-mile from the Lund residence. Anna would have been impressed by this woman's patriotism.

Spencer, Winnie – 10 April 1918

Anna mentions that she "visited Winnie & Marva Spencer." Assuming that she meant Winnie and Marva were somehow related, then Winnie might also be residing at 1229 Bryan Ave., a few blocks from the Lund residence. I do not find any newspaper articles about Winnie. Neither in the 1910 nor the 1920 U.S. Census are Spencers residing at 1229 Bryan Ave.

Spooner, Mrs. – 22 June 1918

"[S]ewed on Mrs. B.'s dress. She & Mrs. Spooner came." Mrs. Spooner must have been a colleague of Mrs. Byerline, either from work or some social group. The 1918 city directory lists several women named Spooner. One is Gladys M. Spooner who was a stenographer for a downtown mortgage company, with the same occupation as Mrs. Byerline.

Spurgeon, Thomas – 3 August 1918

"Spent afternoon with a jolly Idaho boy named Thomas Spurgeon." The only references for a Thomas Spurgeon that I can find are in the Idaho Falls and the Salt Lake City newspapers, indicating that a Thomas W Spurgeon from Burley, ID, was enlisted into the Army Medical Dept. in Salt Lake City. No hint of a birthplace or birthdate is included.

Stanfield, Joan and Edgar Roy – 14 April 1918

It is difficult to pinpoint who Joan and her husband are. However, on 8 June 1918, Anna wrote: "Then out to Saltair with Joan & Eddy Evans & their better halfs." During the week of 7 June, members of the family of Anna's Aunt Evans from Rexburg came to visit, including Joe, Joan, Eddy, and Porky. Two of Anna's mother's sisters married men by the name of Evans. Joan and Eddy were children of Anna's Aunt Alice Partington who married Edward Lovedale Evans. Joe was the son of Aunt Annie Maria Partington, who married Morgan P. Evans. Joan was Anna's first cousin and was married to Edgar Roy Stanfield. I have yet to identify who in the family was known as Porky.

Steward, Isabell – 4 February 1918

I found a 26-year-old single woman named Isabel Steward listed in the Salt Lake City directory for 1918, boarding at 1182 Browning Ave. and working as a stenographer. This address is about one-fourth mile from Anna's house, making Isabell a likely member of the same ward and with the same occupation as a stenographer. This person died 3 January1929 after a year of treatment for encephalitis lethargica, a devastating disease that had spread around the world as a pandemic from 1914 to 1926 and killed roughly 1.3 million people. She was a member of the LDS church, which adds to the likelihood that this was Anna's friend. It is curious that an obituary does not appear in any local newspaper.

Stewart, Shirley – 6 June 1918

"Re'cd a letter from Shirley Stewart of the Coast Artillary." Later in her diary Anna mentions that Shirley Steward is attached to the Coast Artillery in California, although she does not mention which battery he belongs to. She indicates that she met him at the train depot when he was on his way elsewhere, perhaps coming from the East on his way to California. Two batteries were on the West Coast, one in Los Angeles and the other in San Francisco. I do not have sufficient details to identify Shirley Stewart.

Mr. Stolls – 8 September 1918

"Mr. Stolls called while I was gone." A Carter Stools from Ohio, born in Kentucky in 1897, is listed in the WWI draft registration records and fits the criteria here. However, he is missing from the V.A. Master Index, which means I cannot validate his service at Fort Douglas.

Taggarts – 1 August 1918

"I walked up to Byerline's then to Taggart's." The only Taggart family within Anna's walking distance was the Henry and Mary Taggart family residing at 1346 Lincoln Ave, about a half-mile away. It is likely that Mary was one of Anna's clients, although they had a son, Milton, who was a year younger than Anna. They were members of the Mormon Church.

Thomas, Dr. – 21 June 1918

Three dentists named Thomas are listed in the 1918 City Directory, two of which were within one block of where Anna worked. One was Dr. D. Preston Thomas, and the other was Dr. Jenkyn Thomas.

Tolman, Rufus – 3 August 1918

"Ate our basket lunch with...Rufus Tolman, a cow puncher from Ida." Rufus was easy to identify as a farm boy from rural southeastern Idaho, born 3 September 1889. It is curious to note that his draft registration record indicates that he claimed to have a "defective right arm," yet he served in the war. After his WWI service, Rufus Tolman farmed in southeastern Idaho until his death on 2 February 1947.

Trass, Edgar B. – 22 June 1918

"A letter came from Edgar B. Trass." "He is one I met at the depot." This is the only reference to Mr. Trass, and no hint suggests where he was headed on the train. I cannot find any relevant record collections that lists an Edgar B. Trass. Although the spelling of his name may be correct, see Anna's journal entry for Edgar Grass, 10 July.

Vinton, Mr. – 3 August 1918

"Ate our basket lunch with Mr. Vinton...". I cannot identify any person named Vinton or any variation that fits this person in the diary.

Vivian – 5 January 1918

Anna's best friend. Is often referred to in the diary, but never by her full name. She is unlikely to be Vivian Kuhn, because Vivian Kuhn is always referred to with her last name or last initial, probably to distinguish between the two. Once Anna even mentions "the two Vivians." On one occasion Vivian is associated with a Bert, and on another occasion with a Kate. (See listing for P., Viv, page 181.)

It seems that Anna occasionally spends her lunch hour with Vivian, meaning that Vivian may have lived nearer to downtown than to the Lund household. Yet Vivian visits the Lund residence often enough to suggest she lives nearby. I am unable to find an event in which both Vivian and Anna are involved that allows me to locate a record for her.

Watson, D. C. [Superintendent] – 4 January 1918

The second Sunday School superintendent is harder to pinpoint because dozens of Mr. Watsons are in the city directory. At a ward reunion in 1917, the Emerson Ward listed the members of the reception committee, probably the officers of the ward, which included an H. A. LaFount and a D. C. Watson. If the latter is the correct person, it is likely to be David C. Watson, who lived at 829 Harrison Ave, about one-half mile from Anna's house.

Weber, L J. – 8 October 1918

"I wrote a stiff letter to L.J. Weber." This was probably Lawrence J. Weber. See 2 January.

"I saw my old friend in uniform. I am glad to see him thus for I had begun to think Lawrence Weber was a snob." In Anna's scrapbook is a formal portrait of Lawrence Weber in suit and tie.

The most likely Lawrence Weber in the records in Utah was John L. Lawrence, sometimes known as Lawrence J. Weber. Anna referred to him as L. J. Weber on 8 October.

Assuming this is the correct Lawrence Weber: His parents were John L. Weber (1856–1926) and Lizzie A. Moulding (1861–1926).

Lawrence Weber married three times. His first wife was Helen Sheppard Lewis, married on 4 September 1919. In 1922, he married Flora Hannig in Nevada. Two children were born from this marriage, Beth Marie and Sarah Ann. Beth married, but neither one of the two children appear to have had offspring. The third wife was Linnea Celia Erickson, married on 10 November 1939, but by the 1940 census (conducted in April 1940), Lawrence was listed as divorced.

Whitaker, Mr. – 3 October 1918

"The most interesting Southerner who can tell great…stories called on us with his friend. 'Alabama Slim' Coleman Perkins and Mr. Whitaker."

Making an assumption that Mr. Perkins' friend was also from Alabama doesn't help narrow this man down. Thousands of Whitakers from Alabama registered for the draft in WWI.

Wilkinson, Lieut. W. K. E. – 26 January 1918

The poem "At Last Post" has been attributed to Second Lieut. W. K. E. Wilkinson, 1st/8th Battalion, Argyll and Sutherland Highlanders. He died in the trenches on 9 April 1917 and is buried in Roclincourt Military Cemetery, France.

Williams, Fred – 1 November 1918

"Well we went to the party. *We* means Laura, Earl Cushman & Fred Williams & myself." A Fred Williams lived at 942 Princeton Ave., about three-fourths of a mile from Anna. The invitation came from Earl Cushman, who was part of the west side bunch that Anna felt were too young and too soft.

Wills, Walter and Arthur – 20 January 1918

Anna meets Mr. Wills at the ski jump tournament (see ski jump event). He calls four days later, and then on the 25th Anna goes to a church dance with Arthur and Walter Wills. Based on the context, it is likely that Arthur and Walter are related and perhaps they are members of the LDS Church. I found a Wills family that had two sons, Arthur Edward Wills, born 2 November 1892, and Walter G. Wills, born 4 May 1898. The U.S. Veterans Administration (V.A.) Master Index shows both of them as corporals in the 20th Infantry stationed at Fort Douglas. I have traced Walter to his family in Los Angeles, with his wife, Florence Trumble, and two daughters, Winona and Dorothy. They managed a dry cleaning service. Walter died in 1968 at Los Angeles. Arthur and his wife, Elizabeth Conley, can be traced to Riverside County, where they also owned a dry cleaning business and had two children, Edward and James. Arthur died in 1986 at Orange County, California.

Wilson – 24 March 1918

"Layed off long enough to run over to Wilson's for a minute." Anna's comment makes it sound as if the Wilsons resided nearby.

Withem, Mr. – 20 January 1918

Anna encountered Mr. Withem with Walter Wills at the ski jump event. That suggests Mr. Withem might have belonged to the 20th Infantry. I am unable to find a Mr. Withem that comes close to meeting the criteria provided in the diary.

Woodruff, Alta – 27 December 1918

"Alta & Eunice Woodruff were at our house from Smithfield. They are swell old pals." Smithfield, Utah, is a small town north of Salt Lake City in Cache County near the Utah-Idaho border. Alta and Eunice Woodruff were cousins on Anna's mother's Partington line. Eunice was born in 1893 and Alta in 1897.

Woodruff, Eunice – 6 August 1918

"Eunice Woodruff came from [Cache] Valley to see us." Eunice Woodruff was a first cousin on Anna's mother's Partington side of the family, a daughter of Anna's aunt Catherine Amelia Partington.

Woodruff, Le – 28 December 1918

"Le Woodruff met us after and we went to the Odeon to dance." Le Woodruff was probably Leo Woodruff, Alta and Eunice's older brother and another of Anna's cousins.

Woolley, Lawrence – 11 December 1918

"[M]y boss, is very nice to work for. He reminds me of Lawrence

Woolley. No wonder I like him." The only Lawrence Woolley in the 1918 city directory is Lawrence F. Woolley, a soldier living at 860 2nd East, about five miles from Anna's house. If, in fact, this man is Lawrence Foss Woolley, he is the second cousin once removed from my mother, who married one of Anna's sons in 1942. We find no clue how Anna knew Lawrence, or whether my parents knew of that relationship.

Youngberg, Jim – 7 March 1918

Anna mentions meeting Jim when visiting her brother Leander. She said he wanted to go out to the Bingham mine. There is no further mention. It is possible that he was visiting Leander and Ruby from out-of-town and wanted to see a popular tourist site.

NOTES

1. *Deseret Evening News*, Salt Lake City, Utah, 14 July 1917, page 3.

2. Columbia Trust was the newest and smallest savings and loan bank in Salt Lake City. All the other half-dozen savings and loan banks reported total assets in $millions. Columbia Trust's statement was one quarter of a million.

3. Dr. Ernest A. Tripp was a Utah native who shows up in records as a dentist in Salt Lake City as early as 1898. In the 1900 U.S. Census, he was 17 years old and listed as an apprentice to a dentist.

4. Using an online inflation calculator, $6.00 in 1918 would be the equivalent of $25.90 in 2020. Minimum wage in 1918 was 21 cents per hour, or $8.40 for a 40-hour week. Her salary probably reflects the status of women in the workforce.

5. *Owen Wister* (14 July 1860 – 21 July 1938) was an American writer and historian, considered by some to be the "father" of Western fiction. He is best remembered for writing *The Virginian* and a biography of Ulysses S. Grant. Wister's collected writings were published in 11 volumes in 1928.

6. By the end of 1917, Douglas Fairbanks had acted in more than 20 films, the most recent being the silent film *A Modern Musketeer*.

7. The Rialto Theater was located at 272 South Main in Salt Lake City. Today it is named the Off Broadway.

8. By the end of 1917, Theda Bara had made 28 silent films, almost all of which have been lost.

9. Ada Byerline was a stenographer for a machinery company, the Landes & Co., a downtown distributor for heavy trucks, tractors, and trailers. Anna could have seen her occasionally during lunch breaks.

10. Bonneville Park was located at 50 East 9th South in the direction of Fort Douglas from Anna's house.

11. Weather records for 10 and 11 January 1918 show the maximum temperature dropped from 40° F to just above 20° F.

12. Given the time and place, Anna may have been naïve about soldiers holding hands.

13. The Orpheum Theater was a new vaudeville theater also known as the RKO Pantages. It was located at 148 South Main Street. In 1920 it was converted to a movie house.

14. During WWI a training camp in Pulaski County, Arkansas, was called Camp Pike, later to be called Camp Robinson. It was originally the home of the 87th Division and served as a replacement training facility. It also housed up to 4,000 German prisoners of war.

15. An annual ski jumping event took place at Dry Canyon, near the University of Utah. Anna overstated the length of the winning jump. The National Ski Jump record in 1918 was 204 ft. at Steamboat Springs, Colorado.

16. The war poem "At Last Post" has been ascribed to 2nd Lieutenant W. L. Wilkinson, 1st/8th Battalion, Argyll and Sutherland Highlanders. He died 9 April 1917; he is buried in Roclincourt Military Cemetery, France.

17. Anna's references to the park throughout her diary probably refer to Liberty Park, a large park situated about halfway between her house and downtown, where she worked.

18. This reference to a "cute bow" made me think of Charlie Chaplin. But Charlie Chaplin was playing at the Rialto down the street. Given the line-up of talent at the Orpheum, it was probably one of the comic actors Billie Montgomery and George Perry.

19. This is an intriguing entry, but multiple Clarence Petersons were listed in Ogden's City Directory.

20. An epidemic of mumps had raged at Camp Wheeler, Georgia, between October 1917 and March 1918. Nearly a third of the camp of 18,000 men was stricken. It wasn't until the 1930s that mumps was finally understood.

21. A baby blessing is a Mormon rite performed during a church service in which a father or other male friend of the family prays over an infant child for a healthy and happy life. It is essentially the means to record the infant's name and birthdate on official LDS church records.

22. "Mutual" refers to the Mormon Church's auxiliary organization for the youth of the church, which was known as the Mutual Improvement Association, or *Mutual* for short.

23. The SS *Tuscania* was a Cunard luxury liner, named after a town in Italy. The liner was torpedoed on 5 February 1918 by a German U-boat while carrying more than 2,000 American troops to Europe and sank with a loss of more than 200 lives.

24. Billy Boy is Anna's brother William, who was serving in the U.S. Navy aboard the USS *Pittsburgh*.

25. The Odeon was a popular dance hall with orchestra in downtown Salt Lake City that was associated with a dance academy. It was a frequent venue for dance parties held by community organizations.

26. Violet is Anna's younger sister after Laura. At this time she is 13 years old, about 6 ½ years younger than Anna.

27. Vernon and Irene Castle were a well-known husband-and-wife team of ballroom dancers. After serving with distinction as a pilot in the Royal Flying Corps during World War I, Vernon died while on a training flight on 15 February 1918.

28. The Soldier's Club in Salt Lake City occupied the top floor of the Bamberger Building downtown at 161 South Main St. It was intended to provide a pleasant atmosphere for soldiers during their "excursions" downtown and to keep them from going to pool halls and bars.

29. Reference to *Sammys* in WWI literature and media was a colloquialism for *Uncle Sam's Boys*. In the *Stars and Stripes* newspaper, editorials commented that "whatever you do, don't call them 'Sammies' (as in 'Uncle Sammy's Boys')"; they hated that. This ill-conceived term was the brain-child of some aspiring adman who thought it best, once he'd learned how broadly his "Sammies" idea was rejected, that he go unremembered.

30. The Tabernacle is a large meeting hall located at Temple Square in

downtown Salt Lake City. It was built by early Mormon pioneers and completed in 1867. It is widely known for its rounded dome roof and for its acoustics. The seating capacity of the building is 7,000, including the choir area and the balcony.

31. A major dry-goods store in downtown Salt Lake City (corner of Main & Broadway), Walker's carried a wide variety of women's clothing and accessories. It was known for frequent discounted sales.

32. Opened as the Empress Theatre, it was later renamed the Paramount Empress Theatre, Paramount Theatre, and finally Uptown Theatre. Located at 53 South Main, the theater was demolished to make way for the ZCMI Center.

33. This event refers to an alleged imposter Chief White Oak who appears to have tricked many city leaders and the Red Cross into participating in a hoax. An editorial in *Goodwin's Weekly* newspaper (23 March 1918, p. 5) commented: "One could readily overlook the whole affair were it not for the fact that the fair name of the Red Cross has been dragged into the controversy. That is the unfortunate circumstance. Otherwise, we might all enjoy a good laugh at the expense of the governor, the mayor, an exclusive club or two, several enterprising society matrons and misses, and all the other dear folk who so eagerly pushed themselves to the front and got duped for their pains."

34. It is interesting to note that surgery for appendicitis a decade earlier had a high death rate, but surgical procedures pioneered by Robert Tuttle Morris reduced the death rate to less than 2% by 1918.

35. The 1918 Spring Offensive or *Kaiserschlacht* (*Kaiser's Battle*), also known as the Ludendorff Offensive, was a series of German attacks along the Western Front during World War I, beginning on 21 March 1918, which marked the deepest advances by either side since 1914. The Germans had realized that their only remaining chance of victory was to defeat the Allies before the overwhelming human and materiel resources of the United States could be deployed. They also had the temporary advantage in numbers afforded by the nearly 50 divisions freed by the Russian surrender (the Treaty of Brest-Litovsk). The Germans were unable to move supplies and reinforcements fast enough to maintain their advance. The fast-moving stormtroopers leading the attack could not carry enough food and

ammunition to sustain themselves for long, and all the German offensives petered out, in part through lack of supplies.

36. See http://sunrisesunset.com/calendar.asp

37. Camp Dodge was a post near Johnston, Iowa, that was originally built as a training facility for the National Guard. During WWI it was turned over to the federal government for a regional training site.

38. April 6 is the traditional date for the semi-annual general conference of the Mormon Church, which draws thousands to Salt Lake City. The first regular session of the conference would have started on Friday, with the final sessions on Sunday. A review of the April 1918 conference proceedings shows that the leaders of the church were concerned that eggs were being imported from outside Utah when Utah farmers and ranchers easily ought to be able to supply Utah's needs for poultry products.

39. The Third Liberty Loan Act was a liberty bond sold during World War I that helped cover the war expenses of the United States. These bonds were loans taken by the U.S. Government in which they would later pay back the money the citizens spent on the loan. There were two previous loan acts, The Liberty Loan Act and The Second Liberty Loan Act, each giving more money to the U.S. Government to fund the war. The Third Liberty Loan Act was enacted on 5 April 1918.

40. Probably the Eagles Club at 402 South West Temple.

41. An officers and teachers meeting would have been a special session for training Mormon leaders and teachers assigned to run the weekly Sunday School meetings. Conway Ashton was a popular orator throughout Utah from the church Sunday School board.

42. Anna's occasional use of the term "soft" is clearly her modest way to describe amorous or romantic content. I cannot imagine a new "wify" being interested in what John wrote to Anna. Perhaps it was passive aggression.

43. Large city-wide dances were held at the Saltair resort on the shore of the Great Salt Lake. They were designed to spark interest in attracting people to visit the resort during the summer vacation season.

44. This note probably refers to the Lys offensive of 9 through 27 April 1918. Ludendorff hoped to destroy the hard-hit British Army before it

had a chance to recover from the effects of the Somme drive. This was the purpose of a new German attack launched on 9 April 1918 on a narrow front along the Lys River in Flanders. The Germans committed 46 divisions to the assault, and, using Hutier attacks (infiltration or storm trooper attacks) once again, quickly scored a breakthrough. The British situation was desperate for some days. Haig issued his famous "backs to the wall" order and appealed to Foch for reinforcements. The Allied Supreme Commander, convinced that the British could hold their line, refused to commit reserves he was building up in anticipation of the day when the Allies would again be able to seize the initiative. Foch's judgment proved to be correct, and Ludendorff called off the offensive on 29 April.

45. Saltair was a large amusement resort on the edge of the Great Salt Lake about 16 miles from downtown Salt Lake City. It was built by the Mormon Church in 1893 to provide a "wholesome place of recreation," but was sold in 1906. A rail service to the resort opened at the same time. In 1925 Saltair burned to the ground. After it was rebuilt, it never regained its popularity, possibly because other amusement sites opened closer to the city.

46. A popular dress style of the time.

47. Young's Cafe was located at 127 South Main.

48. Evelyn Paramore Radabaugh would have been a girl who grew up in Anna's neighborhood (a few blocks away) and was nearly two years older. She had married about four months earlier at age 21. Anna's aside that she would be sorry to have married at that age is perhaps a hint that she was not expecting to marry soon.

49. In 1918 the Salt Lake City Bees was a Class AA baseball team in the Pacific Coast League. Their ballpark was located at 50 East 9th South. It is interesting to note that the team roster does not include a single player from Utah. However, the ball games reported for this day do not include the Bees. Both games were between private teams and military teams.

50. Probably the Liberty Park Grocery Store at 679 East 9th South run by Marie and William Parker. Today it is a "Fine Chocolate Store."

51. Apparently, the same policy of professional courtesy that exists today required Anna to have a different dentist attend to her dental needs.

52. Due to the war censorship in place, I am unable to locate any reference

to the whereabouts of the USS *Pittsburgh* during the latter part of April 1918, other than it was on submarine patrol duty in the southern Atlantic in cooperation with the British Navy.

53. In the Mormon Church, the main service on the first Sunday of the month is devoted to members of the congregation standing to announce their personal testimonies. Members are encouraged to skip two meals (fast) during that weekend and contribute the equivalent monetary value to a fund for assisting needy families in the congregation.

54. The Mormon First Ward would have been meeting at 758 East 700 South. A Mormon meetinghouse stands at that location today.

55. The typewriter was invented in 1867 by C. Latham Sholes, and by 1918 several manufacturers had effective models on the market, including Underwood, Corona, and Smith.

56. Extant records for the USS *Pittsburgh* do not indicate when the ship arrived in Rio de Janeiro, Brazil (not Argentina); later in the year in Rio, the "Spanish" influenza killed 58 of the ship's crew.

57. *Journey's End* was a newly released war movie starring Ethel Clayton, John Bowers, and Muriel Ostriche, set in the trenches of the British Army.

58. In the *Young Women's Journal* for May 1918, p. 291, is a suggested agenda for a patriotic meeting to be held on May 14, with a theme of "Our Allies." The program focused specifically on Great Britain.

59. In 1867 the Deseret Sunday School Union was organized by Brigham Young to provide instructional services that went beyond the scope of the individual Ward Sunday Schools. For example, a Musical Union was created, and a brass band was formed. A magazine, *Juvenile Instructor*, became its official voice. By 1971 the Union was combined with the regular ward Sunday Schools.

60. Probably a Sunday School teacher's instruction manual.

61. D. & R.G. probably refers to the railroad station where the Denver and Rio Grande passenger depot was located at around 400 West 300 South, where the depot remains today. Today, the restored D. & R. G. Depot houses the Utah State Historical Society, the Division of State History, Utah State Archives, the Office of Museum Services, the Utah Arts Council,

and the Rio Grande Café. Anna's canteen work would have been feeding soldiers of units en route by rail to other locations.

62. This note refers to the Aisne campaign of 27 May-5 June 1918. The attack fell on the thinly held but formidable terrain along the Aisne River, known as the Chemin des Dames. The original objective of this new offensive was to draw southward the Allied reserves accumulated back of the British sector, in preparation for a final German attempt to destroy the British Army in Flanders. The French and British defenders were taken completely by surprise, and their positions were overrun rapidly on a forty-mile front. The thrust toward Rheims failed, but Soissons was taken, and by 31 May the Germans had reached the outskirts of Chateau-Thierry on the Marne, less than 40 miles from Paris. In the next few days the Germans sought to exploit and expand the deep and exposed salient that they had established. But by 4 June they had been stopped everywhere. Some 27,500 American troops took part in the check of the German advance.

63. Thirty-minute noon-hour organ recitals at the Tabernacle (inaugurated in 1915) were a tradition that still exists today. The first Tabernacle organ was built in 1867 and upgraded several times. In 1915 the organ was rebuilt by the Austin Organ Company.

64. In the Mormon church, Sunday School classes are usually taught by lay individuals who are "called" to be the instructors.

65. Three registrations occurred between 1917 and 1918. The first was held 5 June 1917 for men ages 21-31. The second was held 5 June 1918 for men who turned 21 since the first registration. The third started 12 September 1918 for men ages 18-45.

66. It is not clear if Anna was able to accurately determine the regimental details of her friends. The 20th Infantry had existed since the Civil War, but during World War I from 1911-1917 the regiment remained mostly in the far West where it served as border patrol until assigned to Camp Funston, Kansas, in June 1918.

67. The Coast Artillery Corp was a large group of batteries that had been established after the Spanish-American War to defend the U.S. Atlantic and Pacific coast lines. There were two battery battalions in California, one that covered from San Diego to Los Angeles, and a second that stood watch over San Francisco and northward. There were three that covered the

Atlantic coast. Some of the battalions were sent to France. Anna's entry for June 20 indicates that Shirley Stewart was assigned to the Coast Artillery at California.

68. Joseph Evans, Anna's mother's nephew, from Rexburg, Idaho.

69. Records listed in the *Salt Lake Tribune* on 10 Jun 2013 indicate that the high temperature for that day broke the record for the highest temperature for that day since 1918. A 100-degree temperature in 2013 was recorded at the Salt Lake City International Airport, which was likely to be a bit cooler than downtown. So the record set in 1918, which broke an 18-year record, lasted for 95 years.

70. W.S.S. (War Savings Stamp) drive was another attempt to raise money for the war effort. Utah was challenged to raise $9,000,000 by the end of the year, but well into December, the state had only collected $6,000,000. Perhaps the population in June had been drained of their disposable income when Anna went out fund raising.

71. This was probably the film *Huck and Tom*, released in March 1918 and starring, among others, Jack Pickford and Robert Gordon. The film received lukewarm reviews. According to Wikipedia, *Variety* called it "acceptable," and *Photoplay* described it as "not so fascinating, being an unbelievable mixture of boyish fancy and Brady melodrama."

72. This is Anna's variation of *Gee Wilikers*, which according to the *Urban Dictionary* is a humorous or outdated extension of *gee*, which is a euphemism for *Jesus*.

73. The advertisement in the *Salt Lake Tribune* for the Strand Theatre on this day is for a one-day-only performance of *Les Miserables*. This, of course, featured the character Jean Valjean. Perhaps Anna could not determine the name of the play, or she was awestruck by the performance of the actor.

74. The 20th Infantry had served mostly in the far West where it served as border patrol until assigned to Camp Funston, Kansas, in June 1918. There the regiment trained with the 10th Division in preparation for service in Europe.

75. During the Battle of the Piave River (June 1918), the Austrian Army, at the urging of Germany, made a fast push into Italy, only to be bogged down by outpacing their supply lines. They were forced to stop, allowing Italian

forces to push them back. U.S. troops were brought in to help provide the Italian forces with much-needed supplies.

76. *The Fire Fly of France* was a spy movie starring Walter Reid and based on a novel that had been serialized in the *Saturday Evening Post* the previous year. It is about a young American who manages to acquire important German documents from an aviator called The Fire Fly and turns them over to the Allies, all while winning the love of a beautiful girl.

77. The *Stars and Stripes* is a soldiers' newspaper first published during the Civil War. During WWI, the staff, roving reporters, and illustrators of the *Stars and Stripes* were veteran reporters or young soldiers who would later become major players in the publishing world. Today it operates out of the Pentagon but is editorially separate from it, and its First Amendment protection is safeguarded by the United States Congress.

78. I suspect that a Burglar Scare and a Revolver were items on the menu at Stewarts, although I have not yet been able to verify this.

79. The "Cullen" could be a reference to the Cullen Hotel, the Cullen Ice Cream & Beverage company, or the Cullen Investment company, all present in downtown 1918 Salt Lake City.

80. Camp Kearny, California, was created by the Army in 1917 just north of San Diego on the site of the old Miramar Ranch. Today it is the Marine Corps Air Station Miramar.

81. The closure of the Merchants Bank led to a reorganization to form a new bank, and by the 22nd of the month, new terms were offered depositors to voluntarily transfer their funds to the new bank.

82. The Second Battle of the Marne began on July 15. Because it was a total failure for the German army, it can be considered as the "beginning of the end of the Great War." Allied intelligence was fully aware of the minute details of the impending attack, thus suggesting that the boys "over there" were undergoing intense preparation for a counter-offensive. Military records indicate that 85,000 American troops were involved in the battle, along with French and British troops. A legend proposes that the Germans were tricked into attacking before they were fully prepared, by a clever means of getting fake Allied battle plans into German hands. See historical accounts on the Second Battle of the Marne.

83. Maybe not much to do for Anna, but at about 10 P.M. on 18 July 1918, two large bolts of lightning struck and killed 654 head of sheep on Mill Canyon Peak in American Fork Canyon in the mountains above Salt Lake City.

84. A contemptuous term used to refer to a German, especially a German soldier in WWI and WWII.

85. The USS *San Diego* was an armored cruiser en route from Portsmouth Naval Shipyard to New York City where she was to meet and escort a convoy bound for France. A disabling explosion occurred below the waterline causing the ship to sink in 28 minutes and the loss of six crewmen. At first it was thought to have been caused by a German torpedo, but later determined to have been a mine laid by a German U-boat.

86. A mention in the July 26 issue of the *Mt. Pleasant Pyramid* indicates that 400 Italian soldiers who had been taken prisoners, who had been fighting in Russia with the Austrian Army, passed through Salt Lake City the previous week on their way east to embark for Europe to join the Allied Army.

87. The Battle of Soissons (The Battle of Soissonais and of the Ourcq) was a major counter-offensive fought between 18 and 22 July. It was aimed at the portion of the German Army poised to take Paris. The Allies suffered 125,000 casualties (95,000 French, 13,000 British and 12,000 American), while the Germans suffered 168,000 casualties.

88. Probably a colloquialism for Military Guard House.

89. The boy's band refers to the Military Band of the 145th Field Artillery Regiment, First Battalion. All but four instruments were played by soldiers from the state of Utah.

90. Brigham H. Roberts, later a General Authority of the Mormon Church, was a lieutenant and chaplain in the U.S. Army.

91. Governor Simon Bamberger was German-born and the first non-Mormon governor Utah had ever elected. During the war, he campaigned vigorously throughout the country to solidify the American loyalty of German-born Americans.

92. The band master was Lieutentant Clarence J. Hawkins of Salt Lake

City. As there were dozens of soloists on the program, I am unable to identify the "fat singer."

93. Half-million was an estimate of enemy forces that were about to be trapped by the Allied counter-offensive in the Soissons region.

94. Camp Devins was actually in Ayer, Massachusetts. It had been created during the Civil War but was upgraded in 1917 to fort status. It housed nearly 60,000 troops by May 1918.

95. It is clear that Mrs. Byerline and her daughter, Adelaide, were regular customers. They are first mentioned in the diary on 3 January.

96. This is probably in reference to a newspaper report about German military communications coming through London claiming that the Americans were repulsed from the towns of Fere-en-Tardenois and Ville-en-Tardenois.

97. It is not clear who this Aunt Emma was. The family genealogy records have no one by this name.

98. Eunice Woodruff was a first cousin on Anna's mother's side of the family.

99. A Mormon Church priesthood (male leadership) group that used to function as missionaries in the local communities. Anna's father was a member of this group.

100. Very curious that Anna does not identify the writer of the letter. I wonder if it was from Oswin Rands, who is one of the few whom she mentions being in France.

101. Anna's excitement over the arrival of so many engineers was a bit too exuberant. Only 378 engineers of the 70th Battalion had arrived from Ft. Benjamin Harrison, Indiana, to perform some work on Ft. Douglas.

102. Gossoncourt Woods does not appear on modern maps of France. Either it is misspelled or no longer exists.

103. When the Bolsheviks collapsed on the Eastern front, Germany no longer had allies to occupy the Russians. Allied forces were sent to Siberia to prevent Germany from establishing a foothold there. The U.S. forces included the 27th Infantry Regiment from Manila.

104. Rural farmers in Japan were causing unparalleled riots because of the low prices for rice they were being paid compared with the inflated prices being paid in the cities. In addition, government purchases of large quantities of rice to supply the Japanese troops in Siberia drove prices up further. The crises led to the downfall of the Japanese government.

105. The Conscription Act of 1917 required the registration of all males between the ages of 21 and 30. In August 1918, Congress expanded the age range to 18 and 45, but the final bill passed put the 18-year-olds in a separate class that would not be called up until it was absolutely necessary.

106. Newspaper articles at this time indicated that the War department did not expect the war to conclude any earlier than the end of the fighting season of 1919.

107. A derogatory nickname used by Allied soldiers for a German soldier during WWI and WWII.

108. Don is Anna's youngest brother who had just turned seven years old the previous Saturday.

109. Anna's employer married a 24-year-old woman on 31 August 1918. He was 55 years old.

110. On this date at the Paramount Theatre was playing a film called *The Heart of the Wilds*, starring Elsie Ferguson. Miss Ferguson, a star of Broadway stage and silent films, was billed as one of the most alluring actresses of the day.

111. In commemoration of the success of the Fourth Liberty Loan drive, several hundred patriotically decorated automobiles paraded through the downtown streets of the city for an hour or so, blaring their horns and making as much noise as possible. It appears that this was a practice in many large cities throughout the country.

112. *The Salt Lake Tribune* indicates that on this date there was dancing with a jazz band at the Odeon.

113. O.P.R. is Oswin Percival Rands. This certainly must be the most frustrating entry yet. What could this "souvenir" have been? A helmet? Was she being facetious? No one in the family has any knowledge of a souvenir that Grandpa Dutch sent Anna.

114. Nothing appears in the *Salt Lake Tribune* about military training at the Y.W.C.A., but Colonel Wright seems to be a popular speaker among local groups regarding current military topics.

115. Another evening of dancing to a jazz band.

116. Slang for an unsophisticated person from a rural area; hick.

117. The *Salt Lake Tribune*'s headline for this day: "Huns Launch New Drive for Peace."

118. The front page of the *Salt Lake Tribune* for 8 October carried a column describing the rapid rise of the influenza around the country and mentioning that a few cities were closing all public activities such as schools, churches, cinemas, etc.

119. The *Salt Lake Tribune* for 9 October on the back page mentioned new cases of the influenza in Salt Lake City, and two deaths. The Health Department prohibited funeral services for them, believing that such close proximity to the dead spread the virus. It also recounted the story of the widespread cases reported in the towns of Coalville and Modena in the mountains east of Salt Lake City. No mention was made of closing public activities in Salt Lake City.

120. Surprisingly, but understandably, this is Anna's first reference to the Influenza pandemic of 1918. The first hint of the disease began in January 1918, but because of military censorship of the press everywhere but neutral Spain (hence the name *Spanish Flu*), the severity of the death toll was kept secret to maintain morale. It has been estimated that 50 million to 100 million people died during 1918 and 1919 throughout the world, making it one of the deadliest natural disasters in human history. The first mention of the influenza in the *Salt Lake Tribune* was a small, eight-line note on page nine of the July 3 issue indicating that a Spanish passenger liner arriving at an Atlantic port had fumigated the ship and subjected everyone on board to a thorough examination. In reality, the disease had migrated to Spain from France long after it began.

121. A column on the front page of the *Salt Lake Herald-Republican* announced the closing of all public gatherings.

122. Sugar House is an old neighborhood in the city about a mile south of Anna's home. It is so named because the first efforts to start a sugar beet

industry in Salt Lake City began there. It is also where the first state prison was established.

123. Camp Fremont in California was located in an area around Palo Alto and Menlo Park on the peninsula in the San Francisco Bay Area. It was named after an early California explorer and military hero, John C. Fremont. This reference is probably to the 41st National Guard units on their way to complete their training and head for France.

124. Ft. Winfield Scott was a Civil War-era installation located at the western edge of the Presidio in San Francisco and housed the Coast Artillery Corps battery unit and the headquarters of the Artillery District of San Francisco. Today the highway approach to the Golden Gate Bridge runs through the middle of the old fort.

125. A very popular song first published in 1913.

126. The *Salt Lake Tribune* made no mention of any Halloween activities in the city, but the last few pages of all of the recent issues were peppered with mentions of individuals, parents, children, and soldiers who had succumbed to the influenza. A special column each day was devoted to the tally of deaths in the city and the state, as well as the count of new cases reported to the Red Cross. The only positive aspect of the column was that the number of cases appeared to be on the decline.

127. On the front page of this day's *Salt Lake Tribune* was an article titled, "America Hoaxed on signing of Armistice." The article describes how a dispatch sent from France to United Press and picked up by other news agencies was distributed throughout the country, citing that truce had been signed at 11:00 A.M. and the fighting stopped at 2:00 P.M. The article went on to describe the mass hysteria that occurred in many cities and pointed out that the German delegates had not even reached France yet. The *Tribune* made it clear that its news agency, the Associated Press, had not circulated the false story.

128. Hal was Anna's oldest brother, who married Lauretta Greenwell. Glenna was their two-year-old daughter. Hal and his family eventually moved to Los Angeles, but at this time he would have been 27 years old. His two-year absence might be explained by military service, except the Lund's Service Flag only contained one star. Perhaps he lived elsewhere.

129. Joseph F. Smith, President of the Mormon Church, died on this day.

130. In the Salt Lake City directory are two entries for Dodge Bros. One is a motor company; the other is a vacuum cleaner company. In a later entry, Anna mentions that her boss is a Mr. Dodge, which probably means she is working for the vacuum cleaner company, run by C. R. & W. M. Dodge, located at 535 Constitution Bldg., 34 S. Main—just around the corner from Dr. Tripp's office. See the entry for 24 December.

131. In the Mormon church, the first Sunday of the month is called Fast Sunday and is a time when members are expected to skip (fast) two meals and donate the equivalent cost to the church for the care of the poor. These funds are called fast offerings.

132. Anna's apparent callousness for the plight of civilians in Germany is probably the result of editorial comments that appear in the newspapers. One article tells about how the ex-Kaiser went to great lengths to claim that the war should not be blamed on Germany. Another commentary tried to claim that the lack of food in Germany was not nearly as bad as they were trying to make it sound. Several times comments noted how alarming it was to the civilians in Berlin that the Allied troops were on their way to overtake their city. However, at the same time plenty of articles mentioned German troops withdrawing in an orderly fashion and explained that Allied prisoners of war were being freed quickly and sent by train to the western lines.

133. The *Chambers Slang Dictionary* refers to a *wolloper* as someone who beats up his/her victim.

134. The closing of theatres, churches, dance halls, etc., in Salt Lake City was actually lifted on 9 December, ten days earlier.

135. A lovalier is an ornamental pendant, usually jeweled, worn on a chain around the neck.

136. Smithfield is a small town north of Salt Lake City near the Utah-Idaho border. Its population was about 2,200 in 1918.

137. The Auditorium was a dance hall located at 56 Richards St. This street no longer exists, but the location is where the Salt Lake Convention Center exists today.

138. The Newhouse Hotel was located on Main Street at the southwest corner of 4ᵗʰ South. It appears that this location is a parking lot today.

139. During World War I, the *Louisiana* was employed as a training ship before serving as a convoy escort in late1918. After the war ended that year, she was used to ferry American soldiers back from France.

140. USS *Pittsburgh,* as a symbol of American might and concern, served as flagship for Admiral William B. Caperton, Commander-in-Chief, U.S. Pacific Fleet, during South American patrols and visits during World War I. Cooperating with the British Royal Navy, she scouted for German raiders in the south Atlantic and eastern Pacific. While at Rio de Janeiro in October and November 1918, failure to implement quarantine procedures by Capt. George Bradshaw led to the spread of the deadly strain of "Spanish" influenza on the ship, sickening 663 sailors (80% of the crew) and killing 58 of them.

141. William Edward "Billie" Lund was Anna's older brother by three years.

Topical Index

(All locations are in Salt Lake City, Utah, unless otherwise specified)

Britain: 4 Jul

British: 14 Mar, 27 Mar, 26 Apr, 30 May, Notes 44, 52, 57, 62, 82, 87, 140

broken jaw: Prologue, 8 Feb

Bulgaria: 30 Sep

Burglar Scare: 30 Jun

cabinet maker: Introduction

Cache Valley, UT: 4 Aug, 6 Aug

Calgary, Alberta, Canada: Prologue

camouflage: Prologue

Camp Devins, VA: 27 Jul

Camp Fremont, CA: 28 Feb, 22 Oct, Note 123

Camp George Wright, Spokane, WA: Prologue

Camp Kearny, Linda Vista, CA: Prologue, 8 Jul, Note 80

Camp Mills, NY: Prologue

Camp Pike, AR: 8 Jan, Addresses at the end, Note 14

Canada: Prologue

capitol building (Utah): Prologue, 19 Mar, 24 Jul

census records: 4 Jan, 24 Mar, Postscript, Note 3

Central Powers: 30 Sep

cheer girl: 13 Aug, 14 Aug, Illustration

Chief White Oak: 20 Mar, Note 33

chocolate: 27 Jan, 16 Apr, 5 Sep, 28 Dec, Note 50

church (attended): 6 Jan, 13 Jan, 20 Jan, 27 Jan, 10 Feb, 22 Feb, 3 Mar, 10 Mar, 17 Mar, 24 Mar, 7 Apr, 14 Apr, 5 May, 12 May, 19 May, 26 May, 2 Jun, 9 Jun, 16 Jun, 30 Jun, 21 Jul, 11 Aug, 8 Sep, 22 Sep, 13 Oct (cancelled), 24 Nov (cancelled), 1 Dec (cancelled)

Church of Jesus Christ of Latter-day Saints, The: See Mormon Church

cigarettes: 22 Oct

city directory: Prologue, 4 Jan, Notes 19, 130

Civil War: Introduction, Notes 66, 77, 94, 124

coal: 16 Jan, 31 Mar

Coast Artillery Corps (C.A.C.): Addresses at the end, Notes 67, 124

Columbia Trust: Prologue, Note 2

comics: Prologue, 1 Mar, Note 18

Company M: Prologue

confectionery store: Prologue

court clerk: Prologue

Covina, CA: 29 Jan

D&RG (Denver & Rio Grande Railroad): 6 Jun, 22 Oct, Note 61

dances & dancing: 25 Jan, 5 Feb, 13 Feb, 15 Feb, 22 Feb, 25 Feb, 1 Mar, 5 Mar, 8 Mar, 15 Mar, 8 Apr, 12 Apr, 15 Apr, 19 Apr, 15 May, 1 Jun, 5 Jul, 24 Jul, 28 Aug, 27 Sep, 9 Oct, 10 Oct, 28 Dec, Notes 25, 27, 43, 112, 115, 134, 137

daughters-in-law: Introduction

Daylight Savings Time: 31 Mar, Illustration

death toll: 1 Dec, Note 120

death, Anna's: 9 February 1989 at Glendora, Los Angeles, California (See page before Contents list)

dentist: Prologue, Note 3, 51

depot (railroad): 22 Jun, 28 Jun, 4 Aug, 22 Oct, 29 Oct, Note 61

depot division: 5 Mar

Depression: Prologue

Deseret News: 9 Jan, 3 Feb, 4 Feb, 13 Feb, 22 Feb, 4 Jul, 24 Jul, 30 Jul, Note 1

Deseret Sunday School Songs: 30 Jul

Deseret Sunday School Union: Note 59

dinner: 1 Jan, 4 Jan, 6 Jan, 13 Jan, 20 Jan, 29 Jan, 3 Feb, 10 Feb, 17 Feb, 24 Feb, 11 Mar, 3 Apr, 15 Apr, 18 Apr, 16 May, 16 Jun, 2 Jul, 4 Aug, 14 Aug, 8 Sep, 15 Sep, 29 Sep, 13 Oct, 3 Nov, 10 Nov, 24 Nov, 28 Nov, 5 Dec, 25 Dec, 29 Dec, 31 Dec

diphtheria: 21 Jan

diving bell: Prologue

divorce: Prologue

Dodge Brothers: Prologue, 26 Nov, 11 Dec, Note 130

Dodge, Camp: 2 Apr, Addresses at the end

Douglas Fairbanks: 1 Jan, 7 Jan, 16 Jun, Note 6

draft registration: Prologue, 29 Jan, 22 Jun

Drewel & Travkey: 28 Mar

Dutch: Introduction, Prologue, Note 113

Dutchman: 5 Jan

Eagles: Chapter 1 Intro; 8 Apr, Illustration; 19 Apr; Note 40

education: Introduction, Prologue, 31 Jul

Edwards Air Force Base, CA: Prologue

Elks: Chapter 1 Intro

Emerson Avenue: Prologue, Illustration

Emerson School: Introduction

Emerson Ward: Prologue

Emmett, ID: Prologue

Odeon, The: 13 Feb, 19 Apr, 20 Apr, 10 Sep, 28 Sep, 5 Oct, 28 Dec, 31 Dec, Note 25, 112

office, the: Prologue, Chapter 1 Intro, 12 Mar, 22 Apr, 8 May, 1 Jun, 19 Jun, 20 Jun, 6 Jul, 8 Jul, 3 Sep, 10 Sep, 17 Sep, 8 Oct, 22 Oct, Note 130

Ogden, UT: Introduction, Prologue, 31 Jan, 18 Aug, 11 Oct, Note 19

organ recital: 31 May, 4 Sep, 17 Sep, Note 63

Palace: 30 Jan

Palo Alto, CA: 28 Feb, Note 123

pandemic: Introduction; Prologue; 12 Nov; 20 Dec, Illustration; Note 120

Pantages Theatre: Prologue, Illustrations; 28 Dec; Note 13

parade: Prologue, 26 Feb, 18 May, 21 May, 19 Jul, 2 Sep, 28 Sep, 7 Nov, 9 Nov, Note 111

Paramount theatre: 7 Jan, Illustration; 18 Mar; 16 Jun; Notes 32; 110

Paris, France: 2 Jan, 29 Jun, 28 Jul, 7 Aug, 18 Aug, 12 Dec, Notes 62, 87

park: Prologue, 5 Jan, 29 Jan, 9 Feb, 28 Apr, 19 May, 28 May, 1 Jun, 9 Jun, 16 Jun, 23 Jun, 26 Jun, 5 Jul, 24 Jul, 7 Aug, 11 Aug, 16 Aug, 1 Sep, 18 Sep, 13 Oct, Notes 10, 17, 49, 50

patronymic: Introduction

peace: Prologue, 10 Jan, 6 Oct, 11 Oct, 14 Oct, 21 Oct, 2 Nov, 6 Nov, 7 Nov, 8 Nov, 11 Nov, 28 Nov, 4 Dec, 12 Dec, Note 117

pennies (trolley fares): 6 Feb

photographs: 8 Jan, 9 Jan, 22 Jan, 25 Feb, 8 Mar, 9 Apr, 16 Apr, 1 May, 18 May, 26 May, 21 Jul, 7 Aug, 8 Oct, 3 Nov, 4 Nov, 10 Nov, 18 Nov, 1 Dec, Postscript

Pioneer Day: 24 Jul

postal service: Introduction, Prologue, 13 Feb

president of the Mormon Church: Note 129

prisoner-of-war camp: Introduction, Note 14

prisoners: 19 Jul, Notes 86, 132

Prohibition (Amendment): Chapter 1 Intro

Quorum (12 Apostles): 22 Jan

Quorum (Seventies): 7 Aug

rations: 14 Nov

Red Arrow shoulder patch: Postscript

Red Cross: Prologue, 1 Jan, 1 Mar, 14 Mar, 15 Mar, 26 Apr, 17 May, 18 May, 21 May, 23 May, 13 Jun, 4 Jul, 5 Jul, 19 Jul, 14 Aug, 16 Oct, 21 Oct, 25 Oct, 28 Oct, 4 Nov, Notes 33, 126

Revolver: 30 Jun

Rexburg Standard: Prologue, Postscript

Rexburg, ID: Prologue, 29 Mar, Addresses at the end, Note 68

Rhine River: 15 Jun; 10 Dec; 12 Dec, Map; Postscript

Rialto Theatre: 1 Jan, 2 Jan, Notes 7, 18

rice riots: 19 Aug, Note 104

Ricks Academy: Prologue

RMS Titanic: Prologue

Rockwell Aviation Field, San Diego, CA: Postscript

Royal Navy: Note 140

rubes: 5 Oct, Note 116

Russia: Chapter 1 Intro, 10 Jan, 31 Mar, 15 Aug, Notes 35, 86, 103

salary: 26 Apr, 27 Apr, Note 4

Salt Lake Herald-Republican: 1 Jan, 20 Feb, 8 Apr, 12 Apr, 31 Jul, 28 Aug, 10 Oct, 12 Oct, 20 Dec, 28 Dec, 31 Dec, Note 121

Salt Lake Telegram: Chapter 1 Intro, 20 Jan, 26 Feb, 23 Mar, 22 Apr

Salt Lake Tribune: Chapter 1 Intro, 7 Jan, 10 Jan, 30 Jan, 18 Mar, 26 Apr,

www.ingramcontent.com/pod-product-compliance
Lightning Source LLC
Chambersburg PA
CBHW060047100426
42742CB00014B/2723